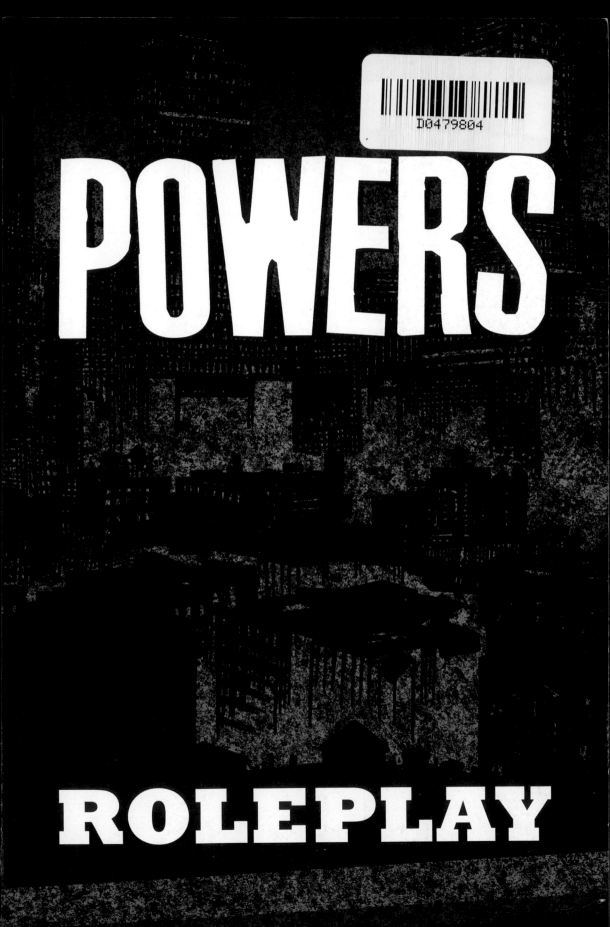

POWERS

ROLEPLAY

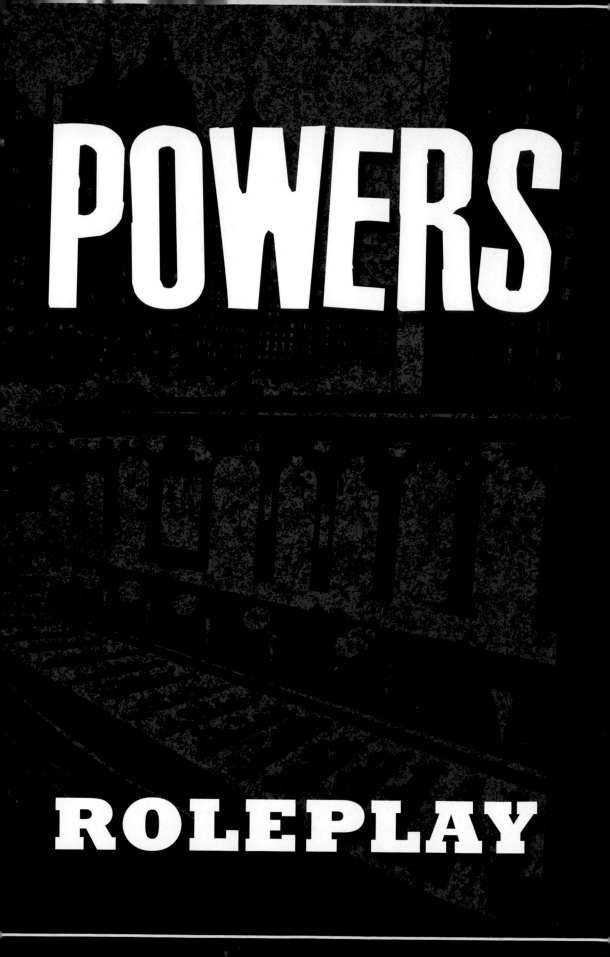

POWERS

ROLEPLAY

Created and Produced by

BRIAN
MICHAEL
BENDIS
&
MICHAEL
AVON
OEMING

Color Art: **PAT GARRAHY**

Separation Assists: **OJO CALIENTE STUDIOS**

Letters: **PAT GARRAHY**

& BRIAN MICHAEL BENDIS

Editor: **K.C. McCRORY**

Collection Editor: **JENNIFER GRÜNWALD**

Book Design: **PATRICK McGRATH**

Cover Design: **TIM DANIEL**

Business Affairs: **ALISA BENDIS**

POWERS VOL. 2: ROLEPLAY. Contains material originally published in magazine form as POWERS VOL. 1 #8-11. Second edition. First printing 2014. ISBN# 978-0-7851-9275-6. Published by MARVEL WORLDWIDE, INC., a subsidiary of MARVEL ENTERTAINMENT, LLC. OFFICE OF PUBLICATION: 135 West 50th Street, New York, NY 10020. Copyright © 2000, 2011 and 2014 Jinxworld, Inc. All rights reserved. Powers, its logo design, and all characters featured in or on this issue and the distinctive names and likenesses thereof, and all related indicia are trademarks of Jinxworld, Inc. ICON and its logos are TM & © Marvel Characters, Inc. No similarity between any of the names, characters, persons, and/or institutions in this magazine with those of any living or dead person or institution is intended, and any such similarity that may exist is purely coincidental. ICON and the Icon logos are trademarks of Marvel Characters, Inc. **Printed in the U.S.A. Manufactured between 8/27/14 and 9/29/14 by R.R. DONNELLEY, INC., SALEM, VA, USA.**

10 9 8 7 6 5 4 3 2 1

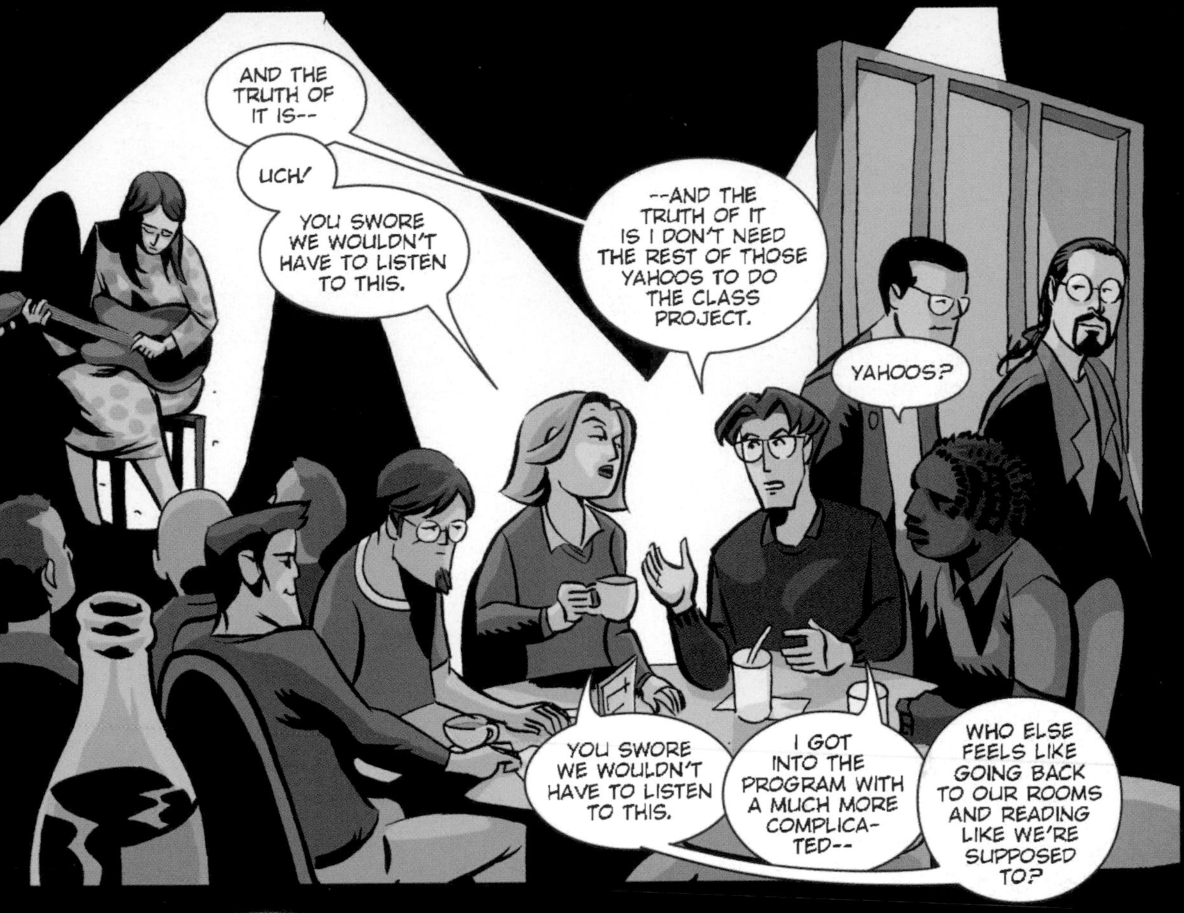
AND THE TRUTH OF IT IS--
UCH!
YOU SWORE WE WOULDN'T HAVE TO LISTEN TO THIS.
--AND THE TRUTH OF IT IS I DON'T NEED THE REST OF THOSE YAHOOS TO DO THE CLASS PROJECT.
YAHOOS?
YOU SWORE WE WOULDN'T HAVE TO LISTEN TO THIS.
I GOT INTO THE PROGRAM WITH A MUCH MORE COMPLICA-TED--
WHO ELSE FEELS LIKE GOING BACK TO OUR ROOMS AND READING LIKE WE'RE SUPPOSED TO?

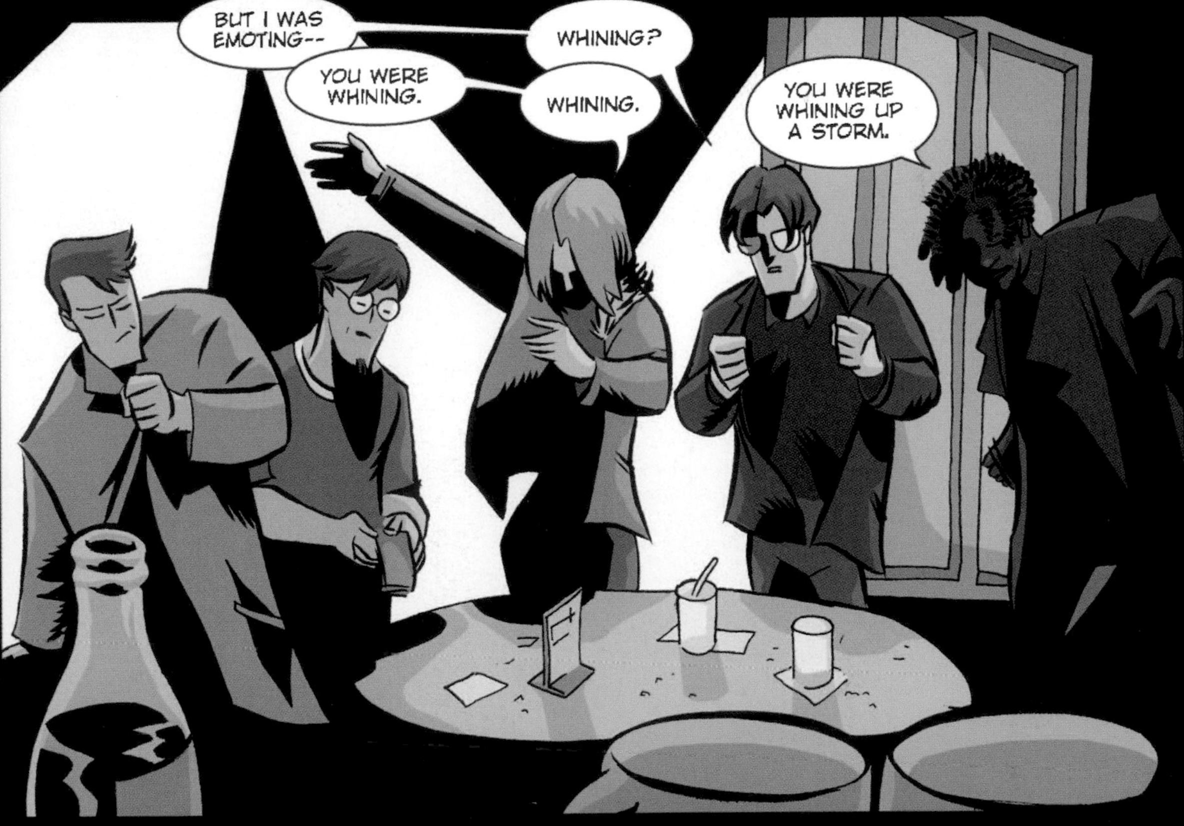
BUT I WAS EMOTING--
WHINING?
YOU WERE WHINING.
WHINING.
YOU WERE WHINING UP A STORM.

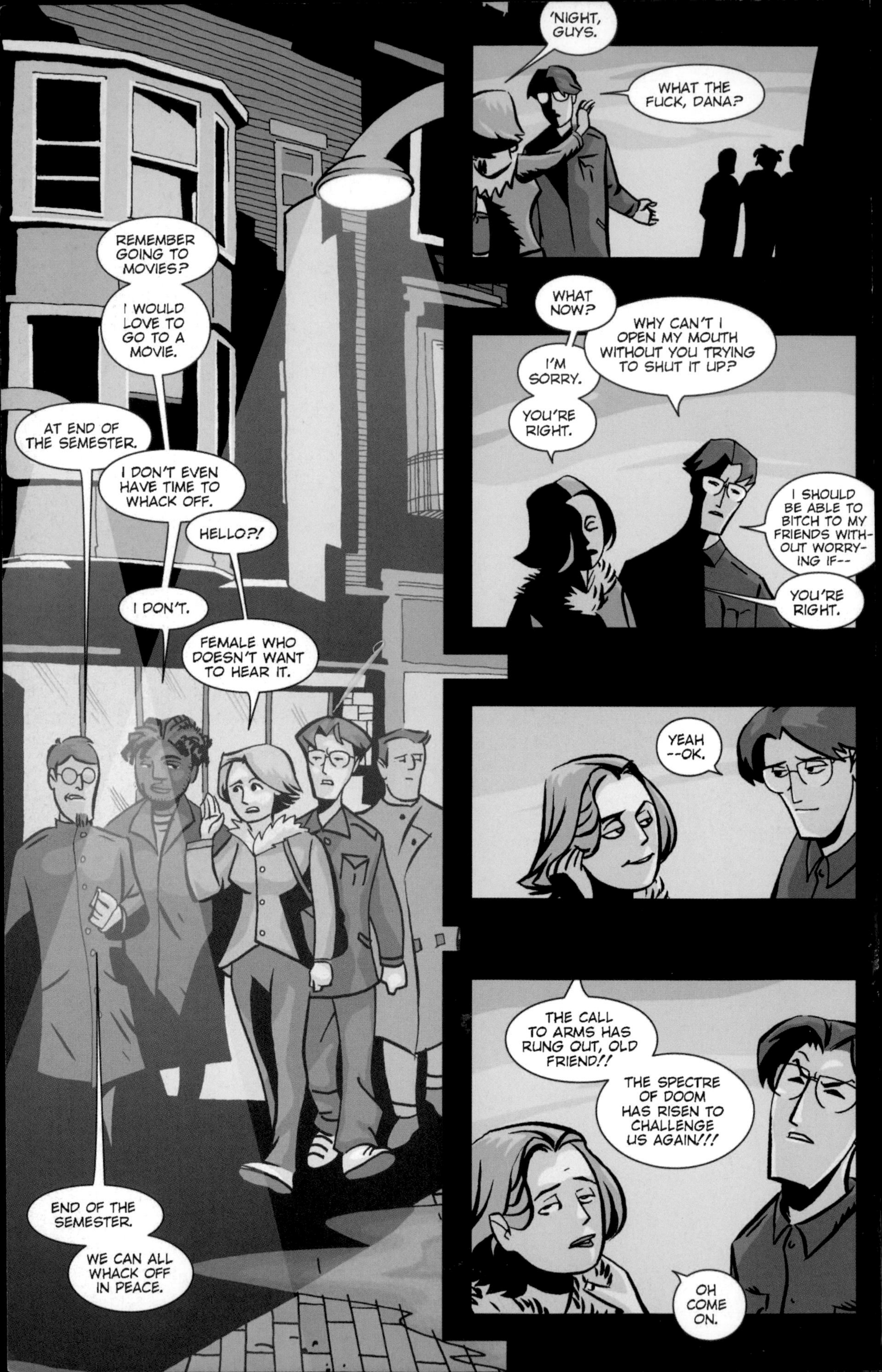
REMEMBER GOING TO MOVIES?
I WOULD LOVE TO GO TO A MOVIE.
AT END OF THE SEMESTER.
I DON'T EVEN HAVE TIME TO WHACK OFF.
HELLO?!
I DON'T.
FEMALE WHO DOESN'T WANT TO HEAR IT.
END OF THE SEMESTER.
WE CAN ALL WHACK OFF IN PEACE.
'NIGHT, GUYS.
WHAT THE FUCK, DANA?
WHAT NOW?
WHY CAN'T I OPEN MY MOUTH WITHOUT YOU TRYING TO SHUT IT UP?
I'M SORRY.
YOU'RE RIGHT.
I SHOULD BE ABLE TO BITCH TO MY FRIENDS WITH-OUT WORRY-ING IF--
YOU'RE RIGHT.
YEAH --OK.
THE CALL TO ARMS HAS RUNG OUT, OLD FRIEND!!
THE SPECTRE OF DOOM HAS RISEN TO CHALLENGE US AGAIN!!!
OH COME ON.

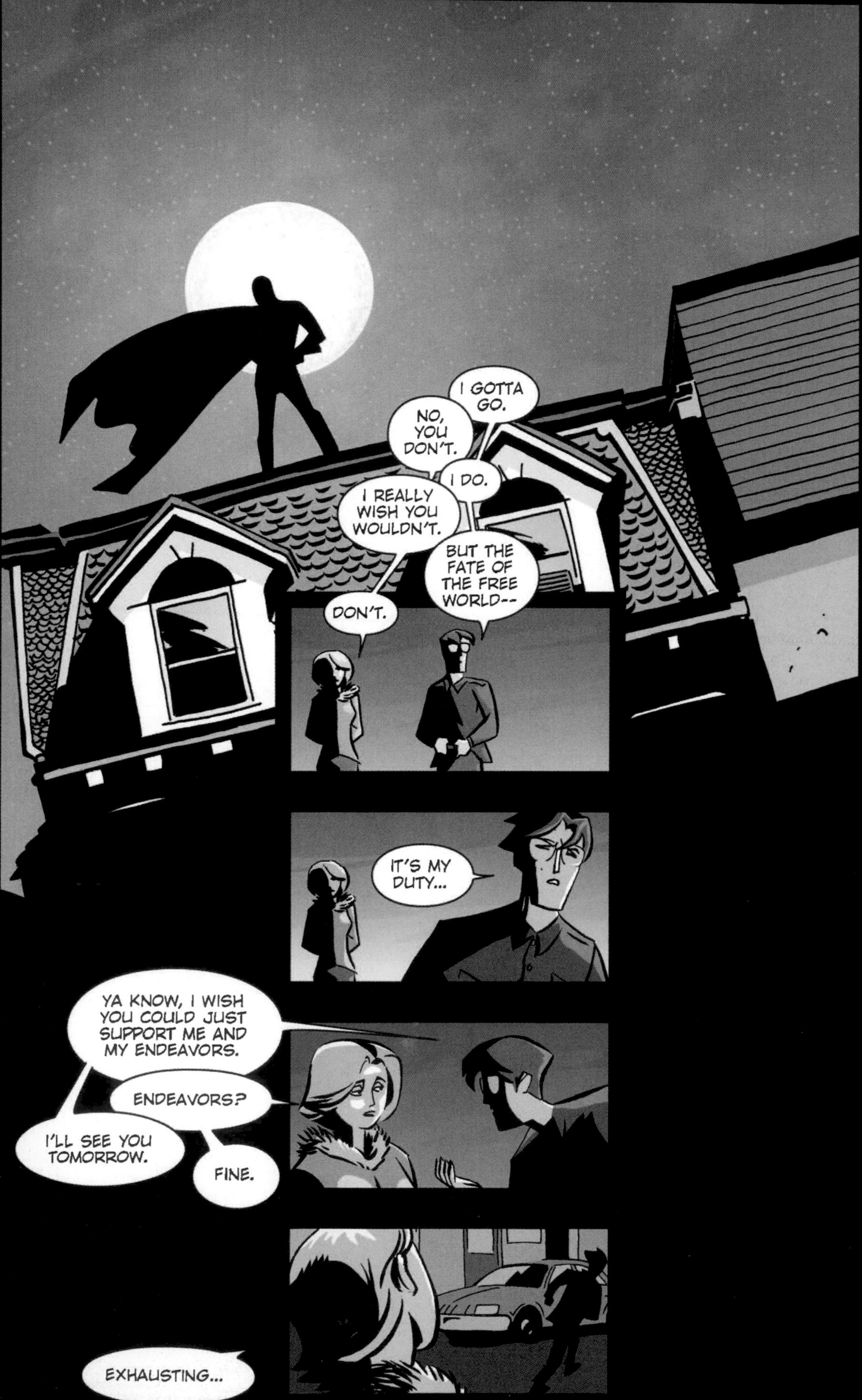
I GOTTA GO.
NO, YOU DON'T.
I DO.
I REALLY WISH YOU WOULDN'T.
BUT THE FATE OF THE FREE WORLD--
DON'T.
IT'S MY DUTY...
YA KNOW, I WISH YOU COULD JUST SUPPORT ME AND MY ENDEAVORS.
ENDEAVORS?
I'LL SEE YOU TOMORROW.
FINE.
EXHAUSTING...

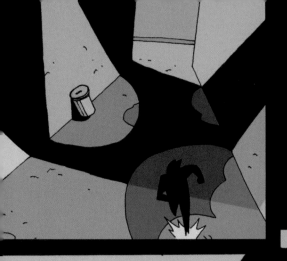

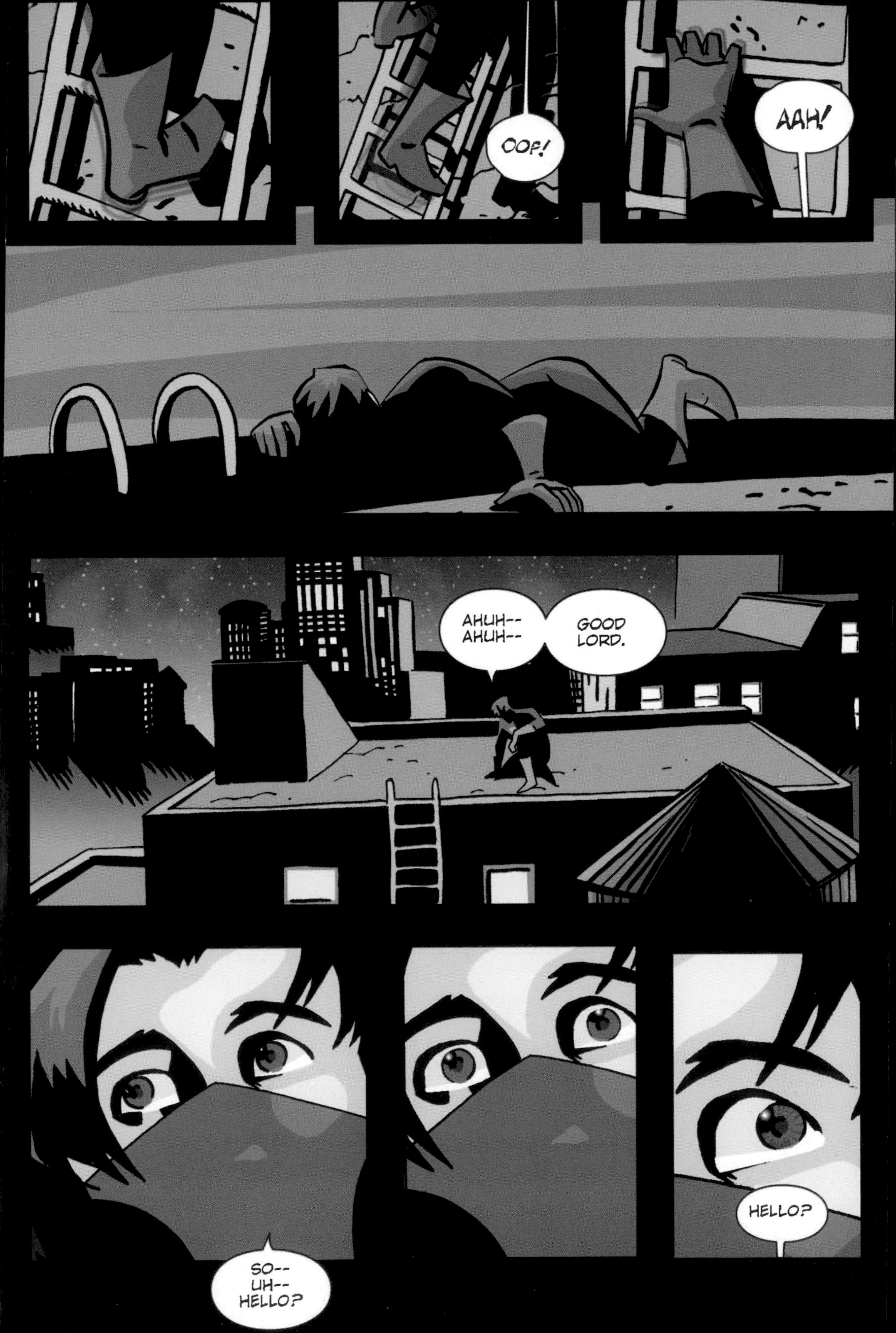
OOF!
AAH!
AHUH--
AHUH--
GOOD
LORD.
SO--
UH--
HELLO?
HELLO?

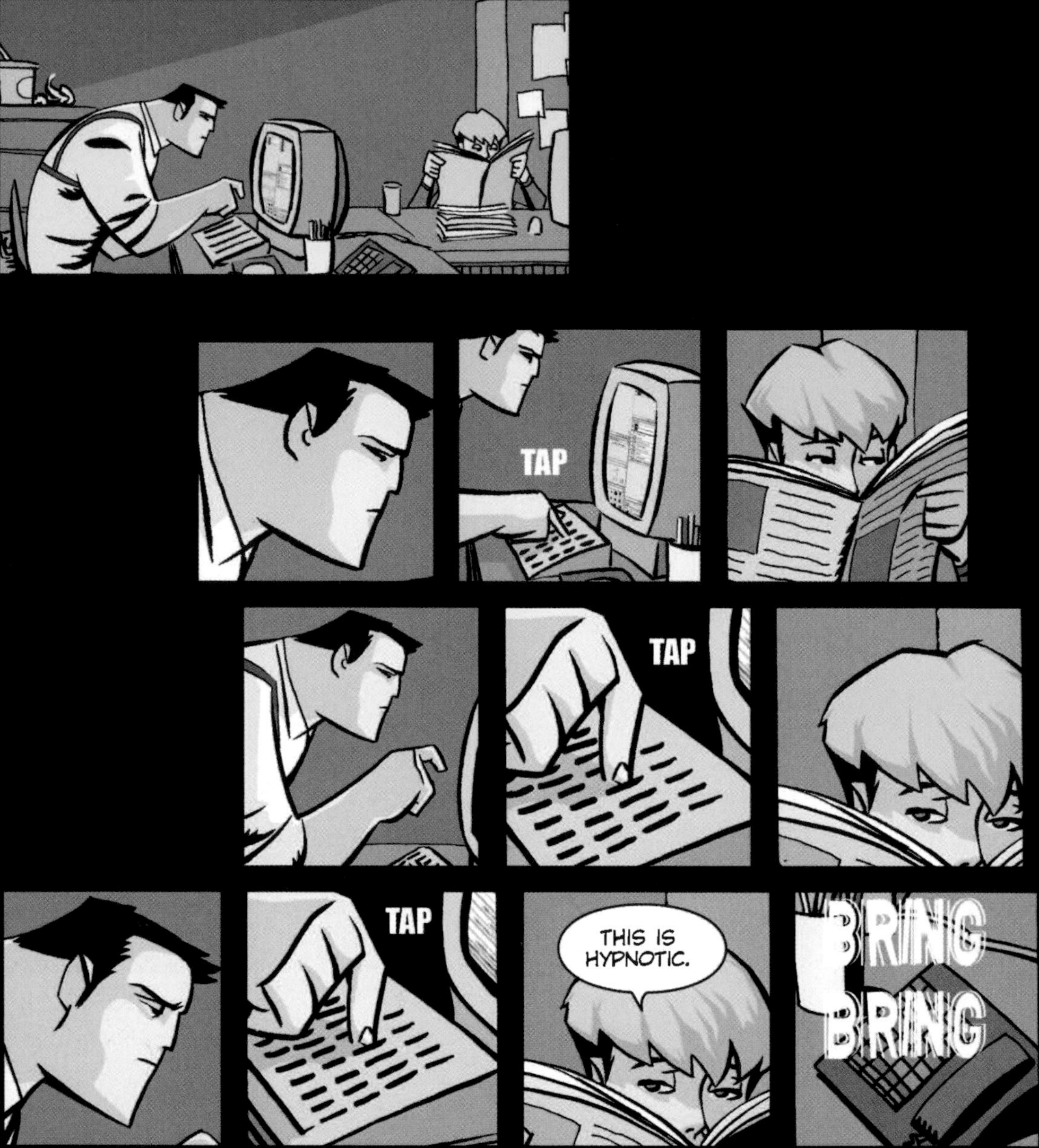
TAP
TAP
TAP
THIS IS HYPNOTIC.
BRING BRING

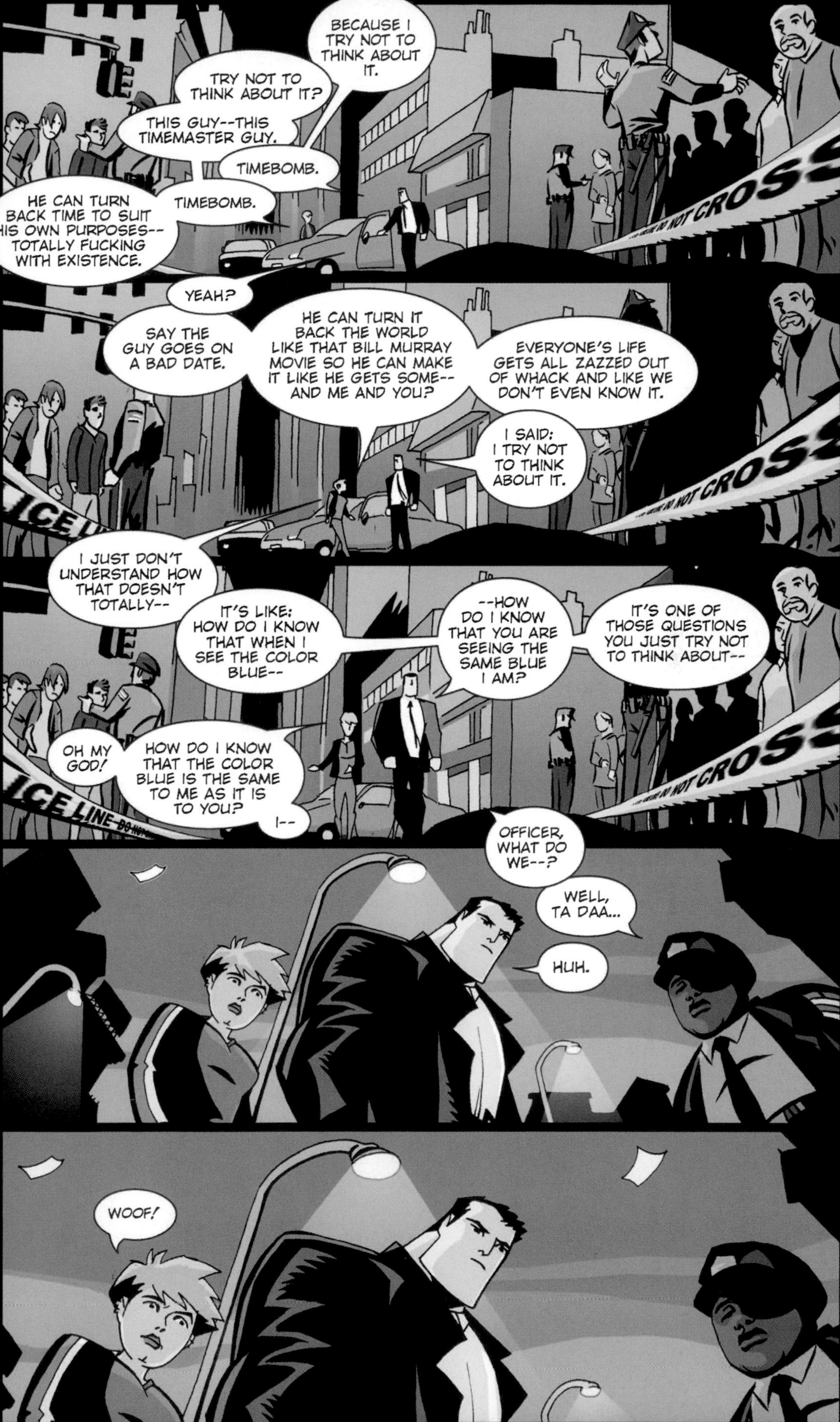
THIS GUY--THIS TIMEMASTER GUY.
TIMEBOMB.
TIMEBOMB.
HE CAN TURN BACK TIME TO SUIT HIS OWN PURPOSES-- TOTALLY FUCKING WITH EXISTENCE.
TRY NOT TO THINK ABOUT IT?
BECAUSE I TRY NOT TO THINK ABOUT IT.
DO NOT CROSS
YEAH?
SAY THE GUY GOES ON A BAD DATE.
HE CAN TURN IT BACK THE WORLD LIKE THAT BILL MURRAY MOVIE SO HE CAN MAKE IT LIKE HE GETS SOME-- AND ME AND YOU?
EVERYONE'S LIFE GETS ALL ZAZZED OUT OF WHACK AND LIKE WE DON'T EVEN KNOW IT.
I SAID: I TRY NOT TO THINK ABOUT IT.
DO NOT CROSS
I JUST DON'T UNDERSTAND HOW THAT DOESN'T TOTALLY--
IT'S LIKE: HOW DO I KNOW THAT WHEN I SEE THE COLOR BLUE--
--HOW DO I KNOW THAT YOU ARE SEEING THE SAME BLUE I AM?
IT'S ONE OF THOSE QUESTIONS YOU JUST TRY NOT TO THINK ABOUT--
OH MY GOD!
HOW DO I KNOW THAT THE COLOR BLUE IS THE SAME TO ME AS IT IS TO YOU?
I--
DO NOT CROSS
OFFICER, WHAT DO WE--?
WELL, TA DAA...
HUH.
WOOF!

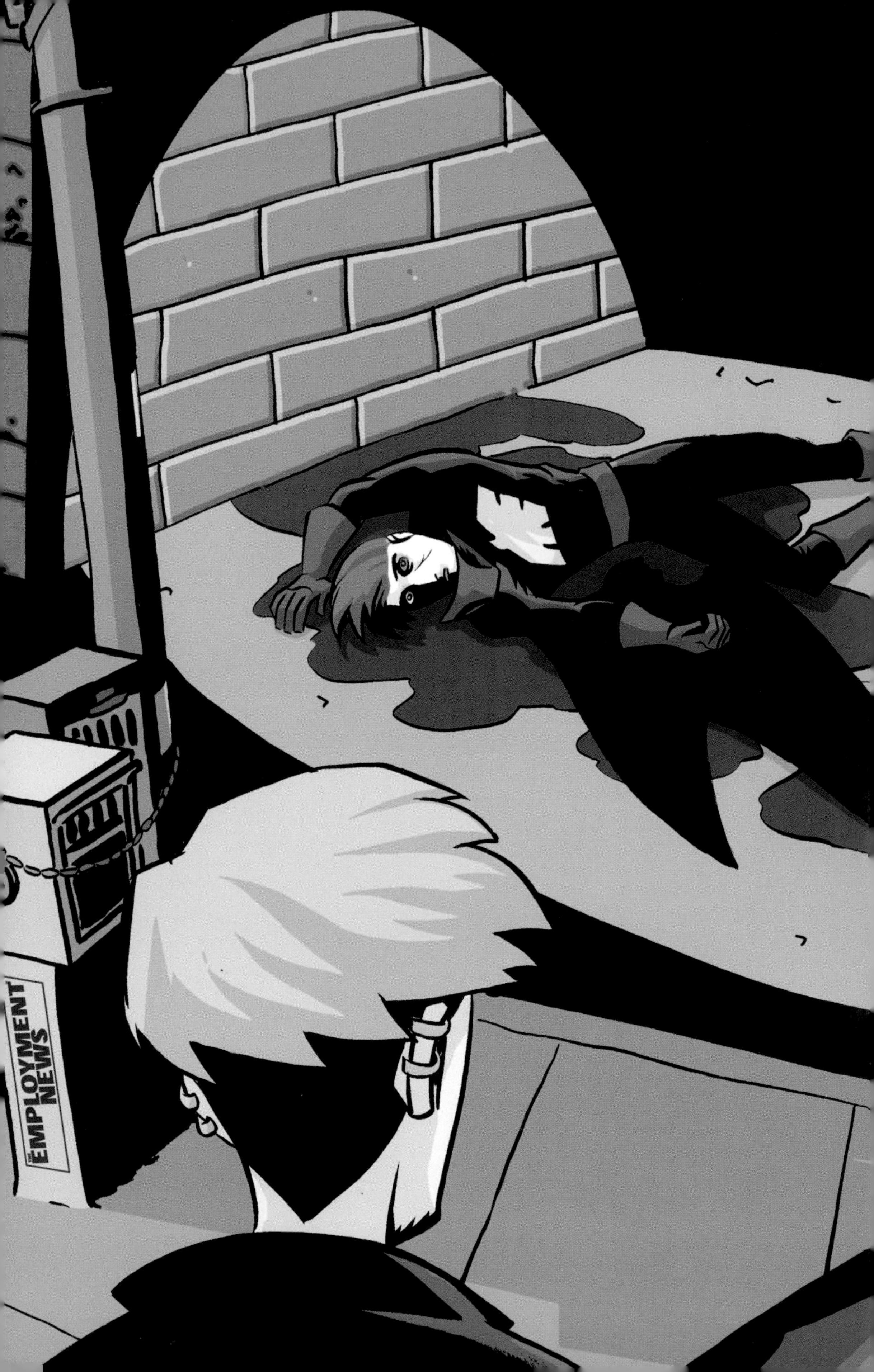
THE EMPLOYMENT NEWS

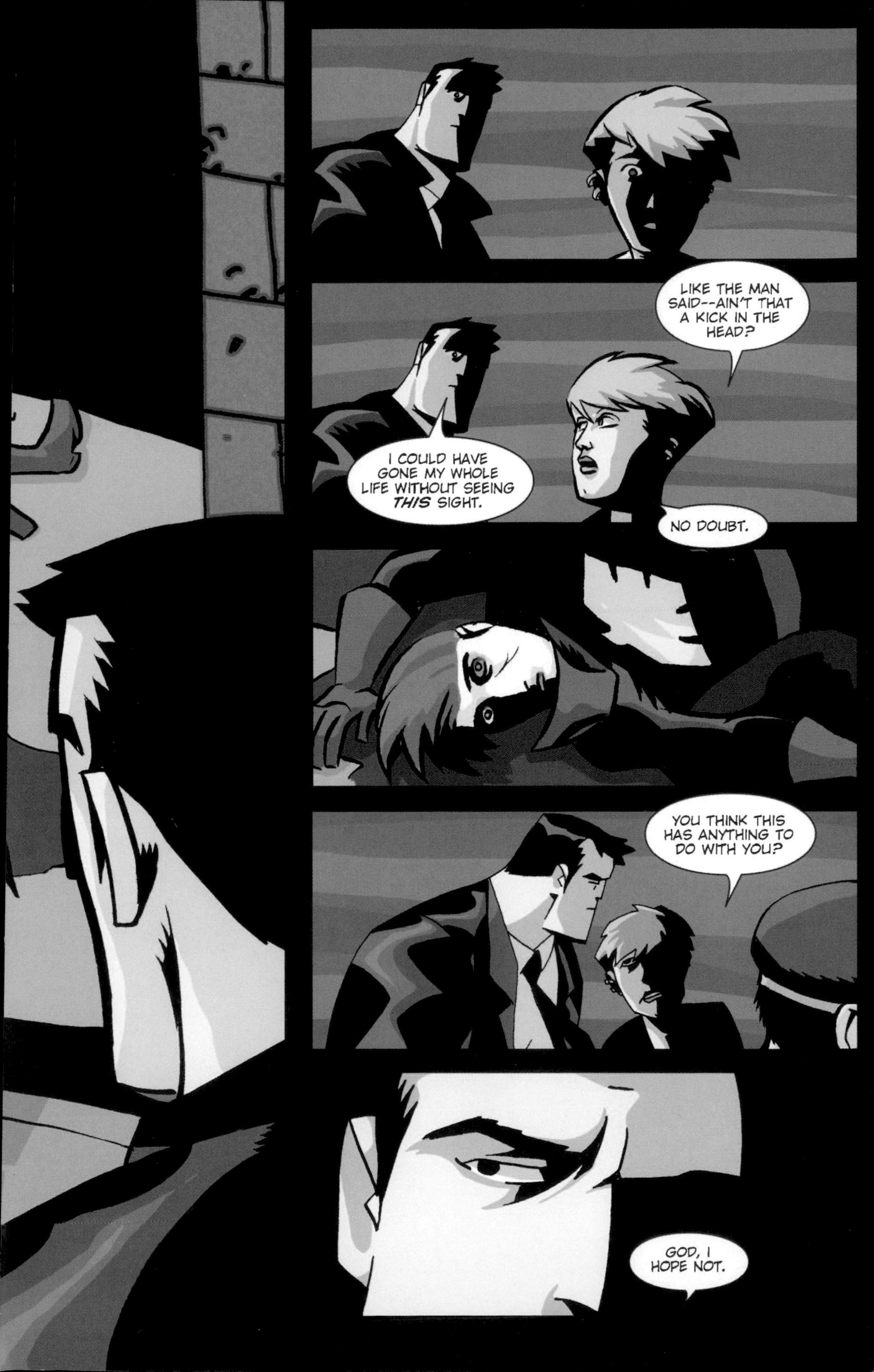
LIKE THE MAN SAID--AIN'T THAT A KICK IN THE HEAD?
I COULD HAVE GONE MY WHOLE LIFE WITHOUT SEEING *THIS* SIGHT.
NO DOUBT.
YOU THINK THIS HAS ANYTHING TO DO WITH YOU?
GOD, I HOPE NOT.

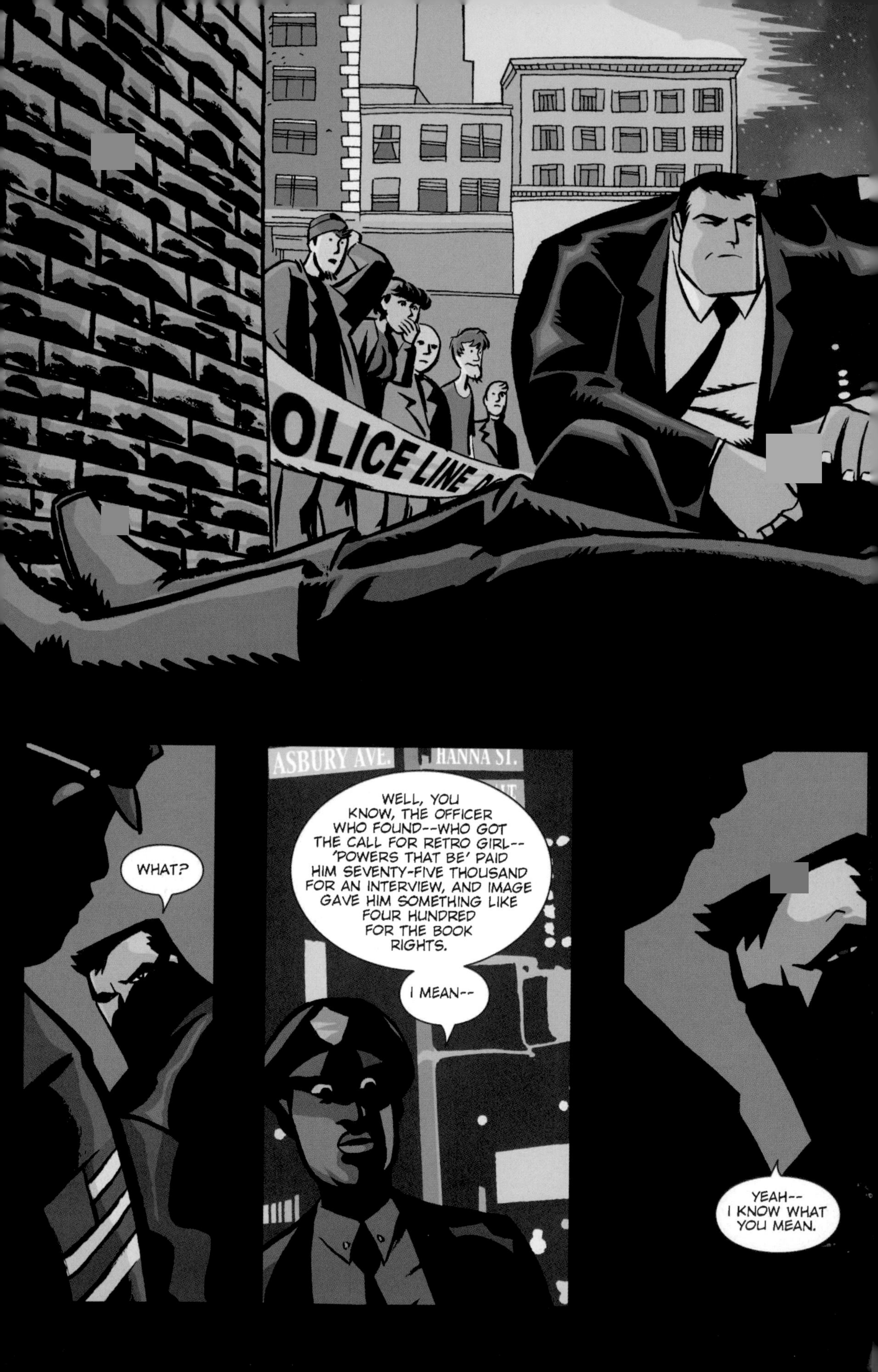
WHAT?
ASBURY AVE.
HANNA ST.
WELL, YOU KNOW, THE OFFICER WHO FOUND--WHO GOT THE CALL FOR RETRO GIRL-- 'POWERS THAT BE' PAID HIM SEVENTY-FIVE THOUSAND FOR AN INTERVIEW, AND IMAGE GAVE HIM SOMETHING LIKE FOUR HUNDRED FOR THE BOOK RIGHTS.
I MEAN--
YEAH-- I KNOW WHAT YOU MEAN.

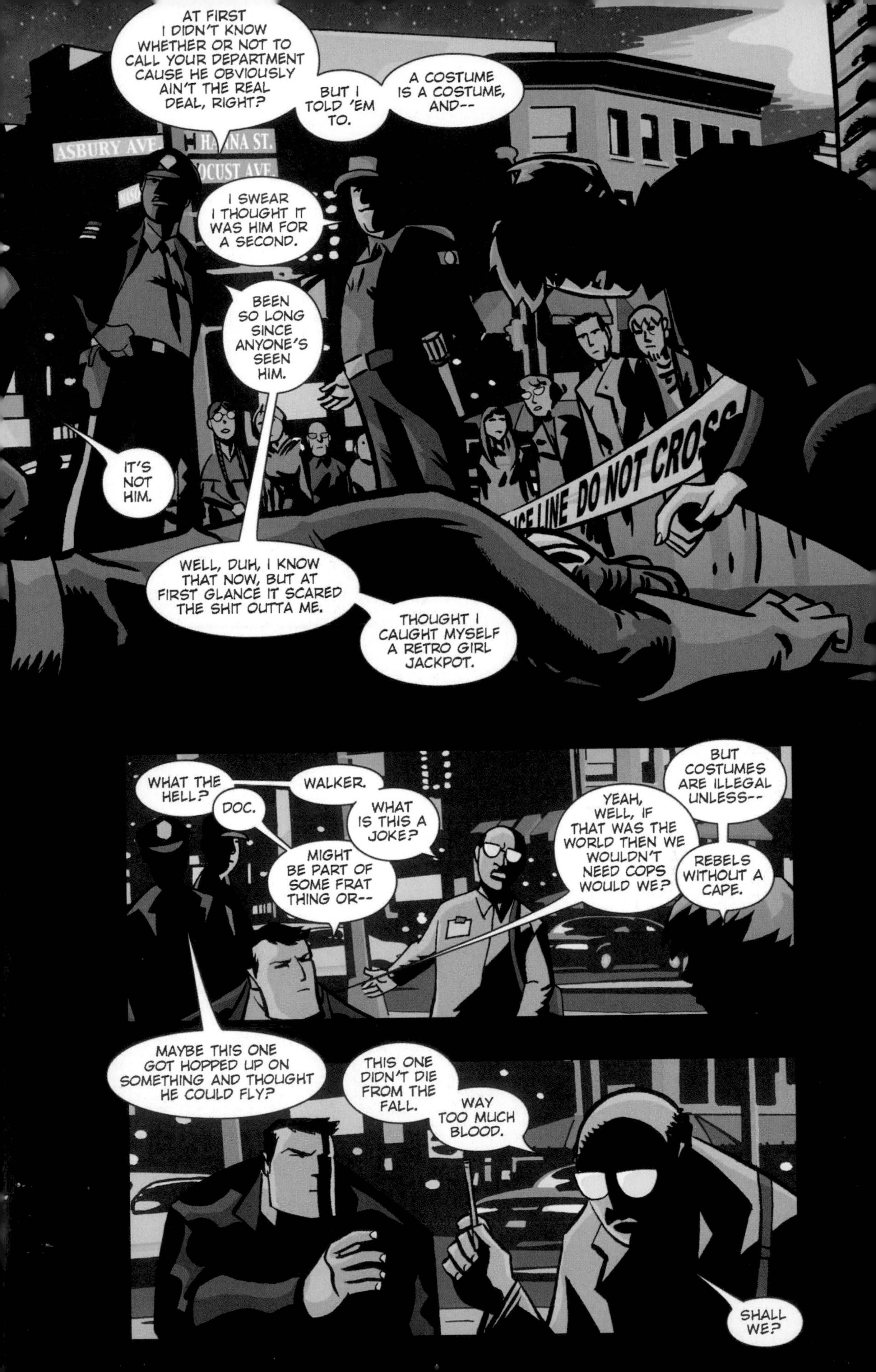
AT FIRST I DIDN'T KNOW WHETHER OR NOT TO CALL YOUR DEPARTMENT CAUSE HE OBVIOUSLY AIN'T THE REAL DEAL, RIGHT?
BUT I TOLD 'EM TO.
A COSTUME IS A COSTUME, AND--
ASBURY AVE.
HANNA ST.
LOCUST AVE.
I SWEAR I THOUGHT IT WAS HIM FOR A SECOND.
BEEN SO LONG SINCE ANYONE'S SEEN HIM.
IT'S NOT HIM.
DO NOT CROSS
WELL, DUH, I KNOW THAT NOW, BUT AT FIRST GLANCE IT SCARED THE SHIT OUTTA ME.
THOUGHT I CAUGHT MYSELF A RETRO GIRL JACKPOT.
WHAT THE HELL?
DOC.
WALKER.
WHAT IS THIS A JOKE?
MIGHT BE PART OF SOME FRAT THING OR--
BUT COSTUMES ARE ILLEGAL UNLESS--
YEAH, WELL, IF THAT WAS THE WORLD THEN WE WOULDN'T NEED COPS WOULD WE?
REBELS WITHOUT A CAPE.
MAYBE THIS ONE GOT HOPPED UP ON SOMETHING AND THOUGHT HE COULD FLY?
THIS ONE DIDN'T DIE FROM THE FALL.
WAY TOO MUCH BLOOD.
SHALL WE?

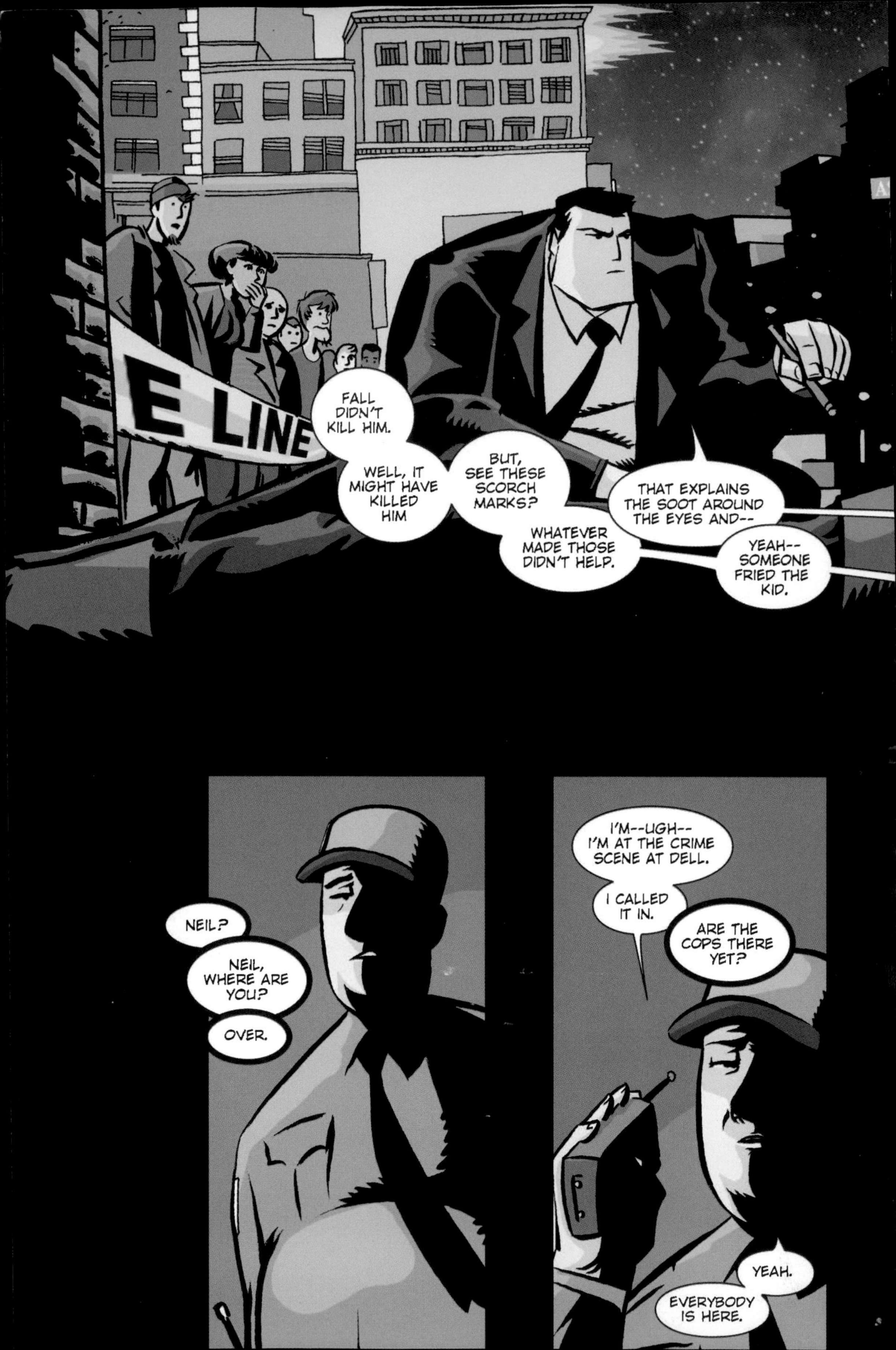
E LINE
FALL DIDN'T KILL HIM.
WELL, IT MIGHT HAVE KILLED HIM
BUT, SEE THESE SCORCH MARKS?
WHATEVER MADE THOSE DIDN'T HELP.
THAT EXPLAINS THE SOOT AROUND THE EYES AND--
YEAH-- SOMEONE FRIED THE KID.
NEIL?
NEIL, WHERE ARE YOU?
OVER.
I'M--UGH-- I'M AT THE CRIME SCENE AT DELL.
I CALLED IT IN.
ARE THE COPS THERE YET?
YEAH.
EVERYBODY IS HERE.

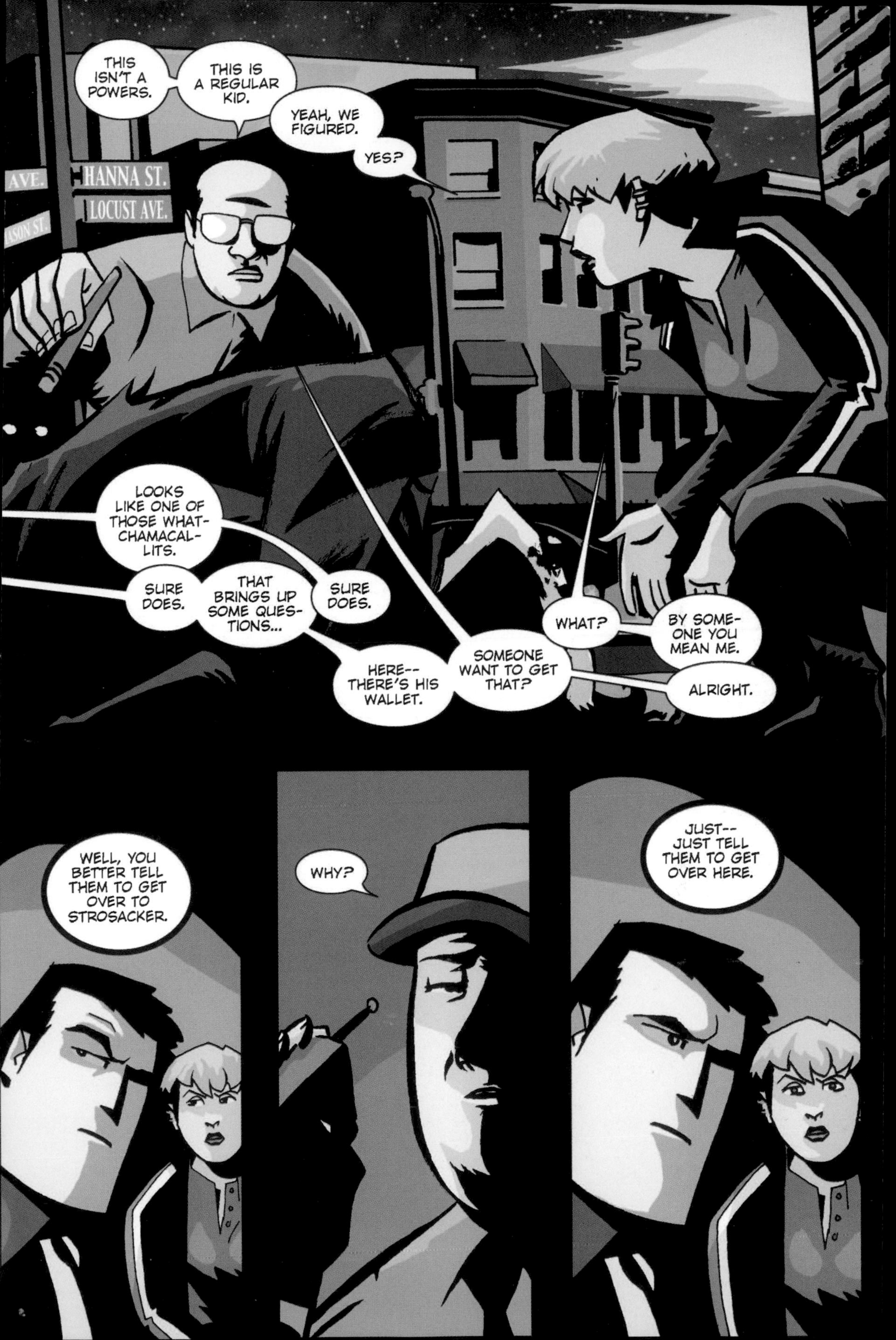
HANNA ST.
LOCUST AVE.
THIS ISN'T A POWERS.
THIS IS A REGULAR KID.
YEAH, WE FIGURED.
YES?
LOOKS LIKE ONE OF THOSE WHAT-CHAMACAL-LITS.
SURE DOES.
SURE DOES.
THAT BRINGS UP SOME QUES-TIONS...
HERE-- THERE'S HIS WALLET.
SOMEONE WANT TO GET THAT?
WHAT?
BY SOME-ONE YOU MEAN ME.
ALRIGHT.
WELL, YOU BETTER TELL THEM TO GET OVER TO STROSACKER.
WHY?
JUST-- JUST TELL THEM TO GET OVER HERE.

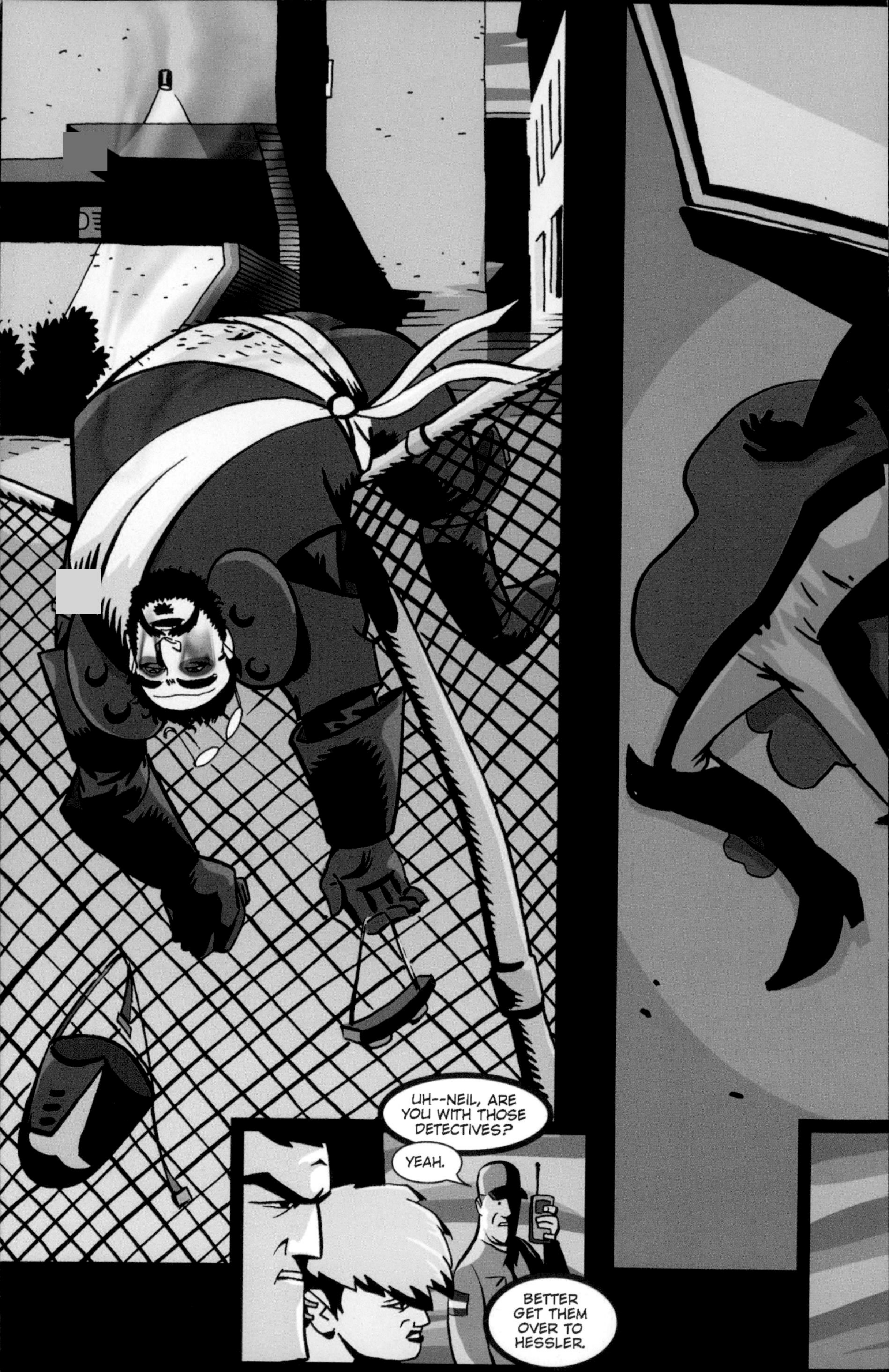
UH--NEIL, ARE YOU WITH THOSE DETECTIVES?
YEAH.
BETTER GET THEM OVER TO HESSLER.

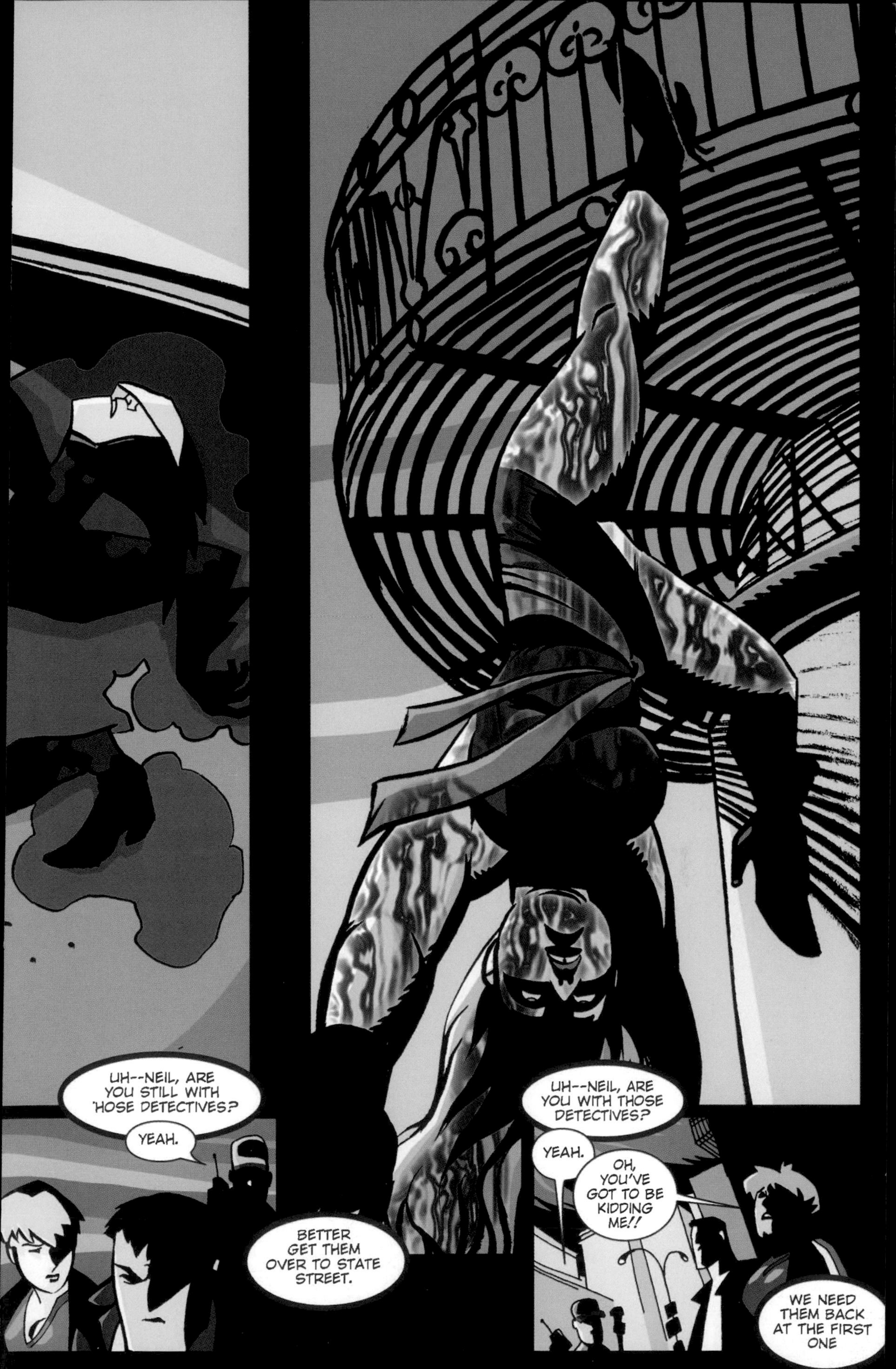
UH--NEIL, ARE YOU STILL WITH THOSE DETECTIVES?
YEAH.
BETTER GET THEM OVER TO STATE STREET.
UH--NEIL, ARE YOU WITH THOSE DETECTIVES?
YEAH.
OH, YOU'VE GOT TO BE KIDDING ME!!
WE NEED THEM BACK AT THE FIRST ONE

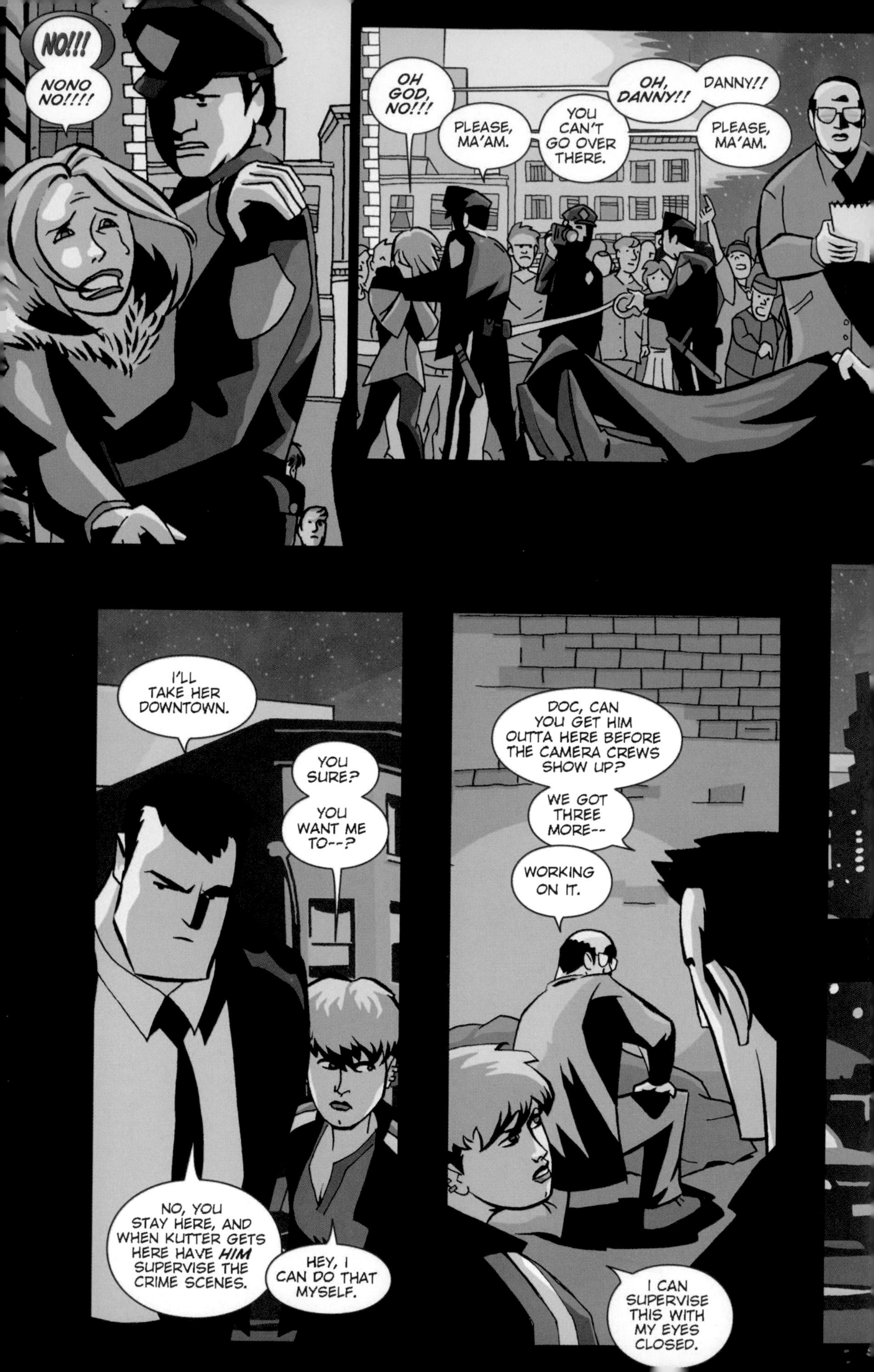
NO!!!
NONO NO!!!!
OH GOD, NO!!!
PLEASE, MA'AM.
YOU CAN'T GO OVER THERE.
OH, DANNY!!
DANNY!!
PLEASE, MA'AM.
I'LL TAKE HER DOWNTOWN.
YOU SURE?
YOU WANT ME TO--?
NO, YOU STAY HERE, AND WHEN KUTTER GETS HERE HAVE HIM SUPERVISE THE CRIME SCENES.
HEY, I CAN DO THAT MYSELF.
DOC, CAN YOU GET HIM OUTTA HERE BEFORE THE CAMERA CREWS SHOW UP?
WE GOT THREE MORE--
WORKING ON IT.
I CAN SUPERVISE THIS WITH MY EYES CLOSED.

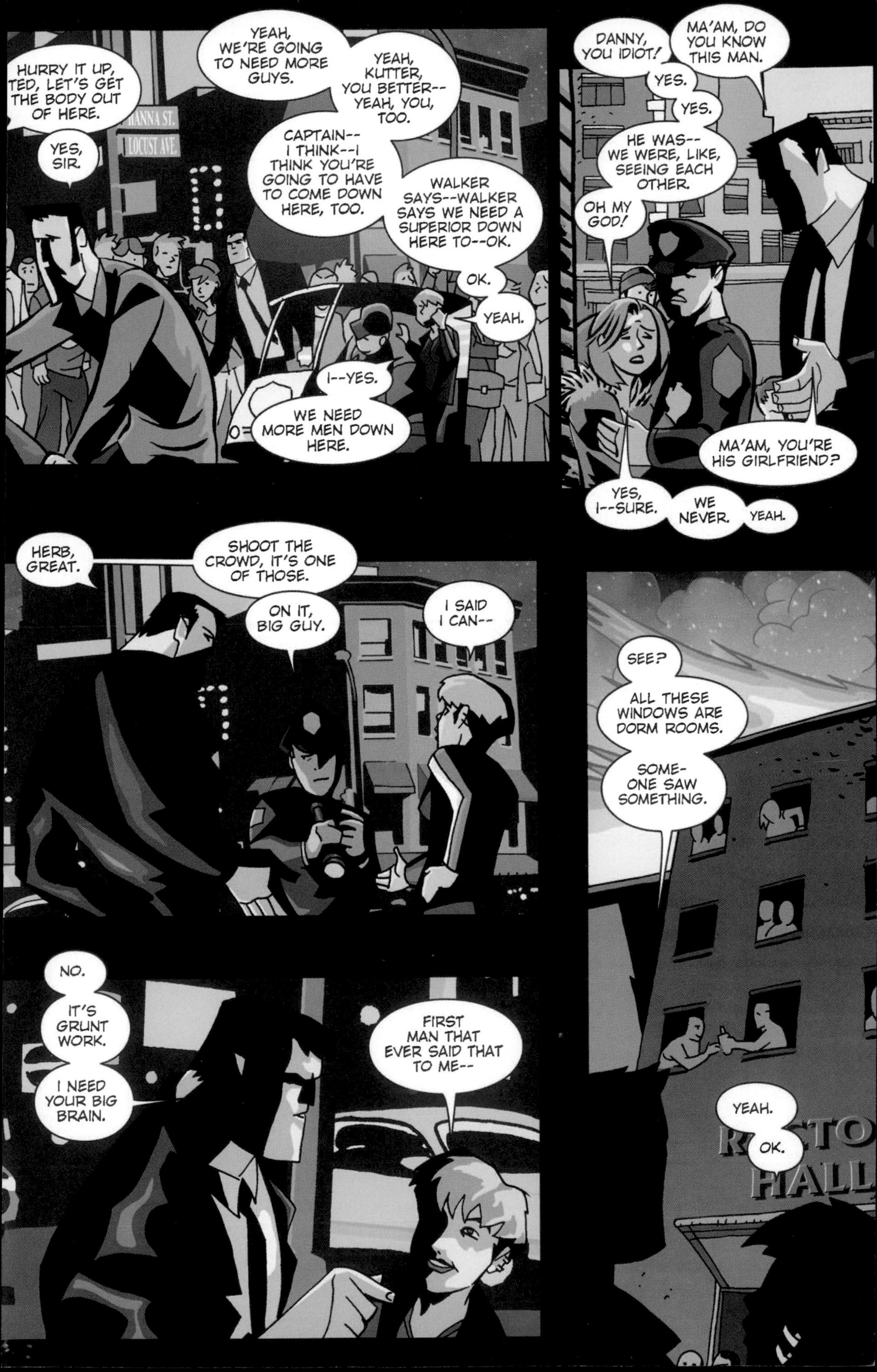
HURRY IT UP, TED, LET'S GET THE BODY OUT OF HERE.
YES, SIR.
YEAH, WE'RE GOING TO NEED MORE GUYS.
YEAH, KUTTER, YOU BETTER-- YEAH, YOU, TOO.
CAPTAIN-- I THINK--I THINK YOU'RE GOING TO HAVE TO COME DOWN HERE, TOO.
WALKER SAYS--WALKER SAYS WE NEED A SUPERIOR DOWN HERE TO--OK.
OK.
YEAH.
I--YES.
WE NEED MORE MEN DOWN HERE.
HANNA ST.
LOCUST AVE.
DANNY, YOU IDIOT!
MA'AM, DO YOU KNOW THIS MAN.
YES.
YES.
HE WAS-- WE WERE, LIKE, SEEING EACH OTHER.
OH MY GOD!
MA'AM, YOU'RE HIS GIRLFRIEND?
YES, I--SURE.
WE NEVER.
YEAH.
HERB, GREAT.
SHOOT THE CROWD, IT'S ONE OF THOSE.
ON IT, BIG GUY.
I SAID I CAN--
NO.
IT'S GRUNT WORK.
I NEED YOUR BIG BRAIN.
FIRST MAN THAT EVER SAID THAT TO ME--
SEE?
ALL THESE WINDOWS ARE DORM ROOMS.
SOME-ONE SAW SOMETHING.
YEAH.
OK.

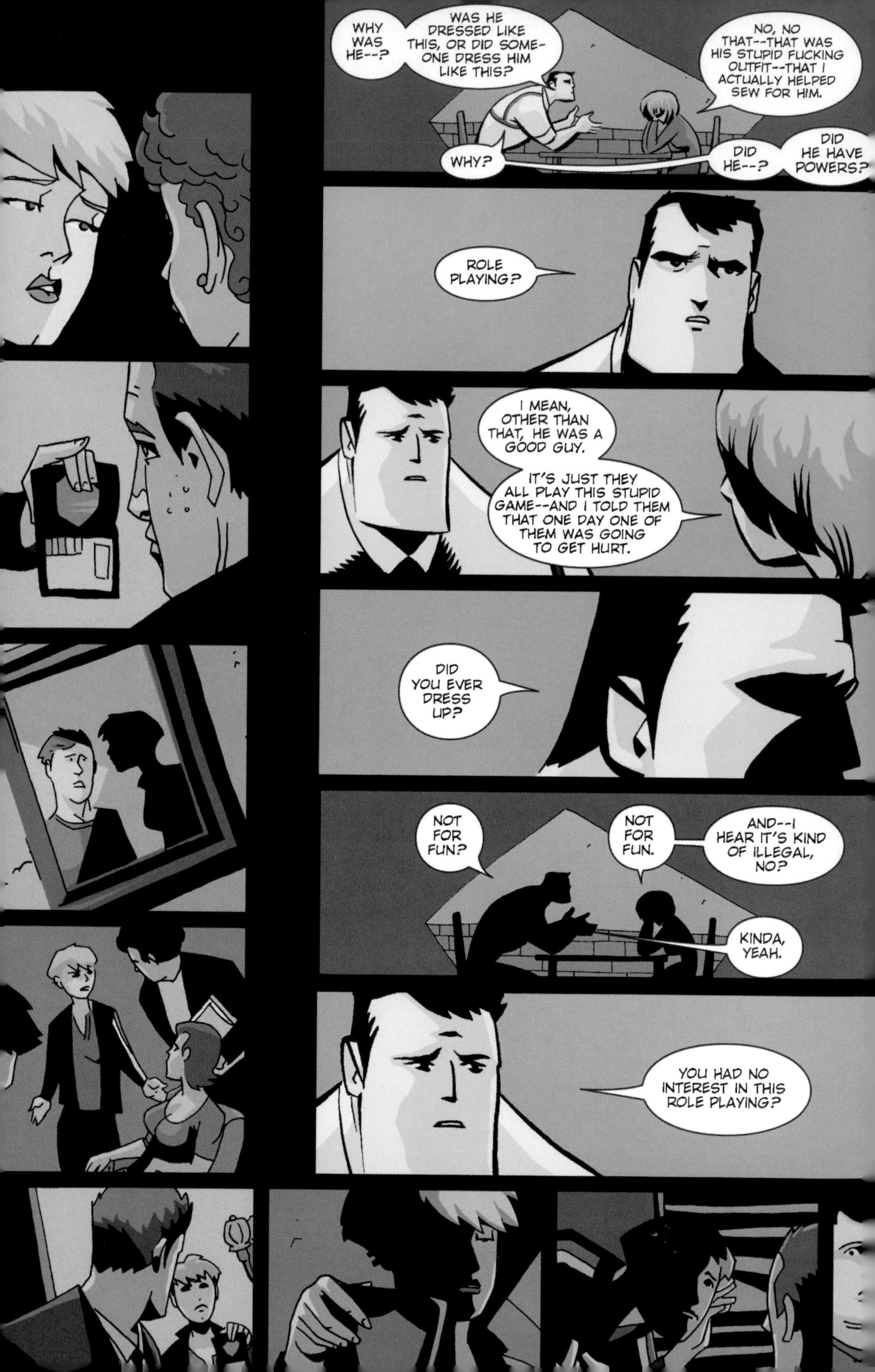
WHY WAS HE--?
WAS HE DRESSED LIKE THIS, OR DID SOME-ONE DRESS HIM LIKE THIS?
NO, NO THAT--THAT WAS HIS STUPID FUCKING OUTFIT--THAT I ACTUALLY HELPED SEW FOR HIM.
WHY?
DID HE--?
DID HE HAVE POWERS?
ROLE PLAYING?
I MEAN, OTHER THAN THAT, HE WAS A GOOD GUY.
IT'S JUST THEY ALL PLAY THIS STUPID GAME--AND I TOLD THEM THAT ONE DAY ONE OF THEM WAS GOING TO GET HURT.
DID YOU EVER DRESS UP?
NOT FOR FUN?
NOT FOR FUN.
AND--I HEAR IT'S KIND OF ILLEGAL, NO?
KINDA, YEAH.
YOU HAD NO INTEREST IN THIS ROLE PLAYING?

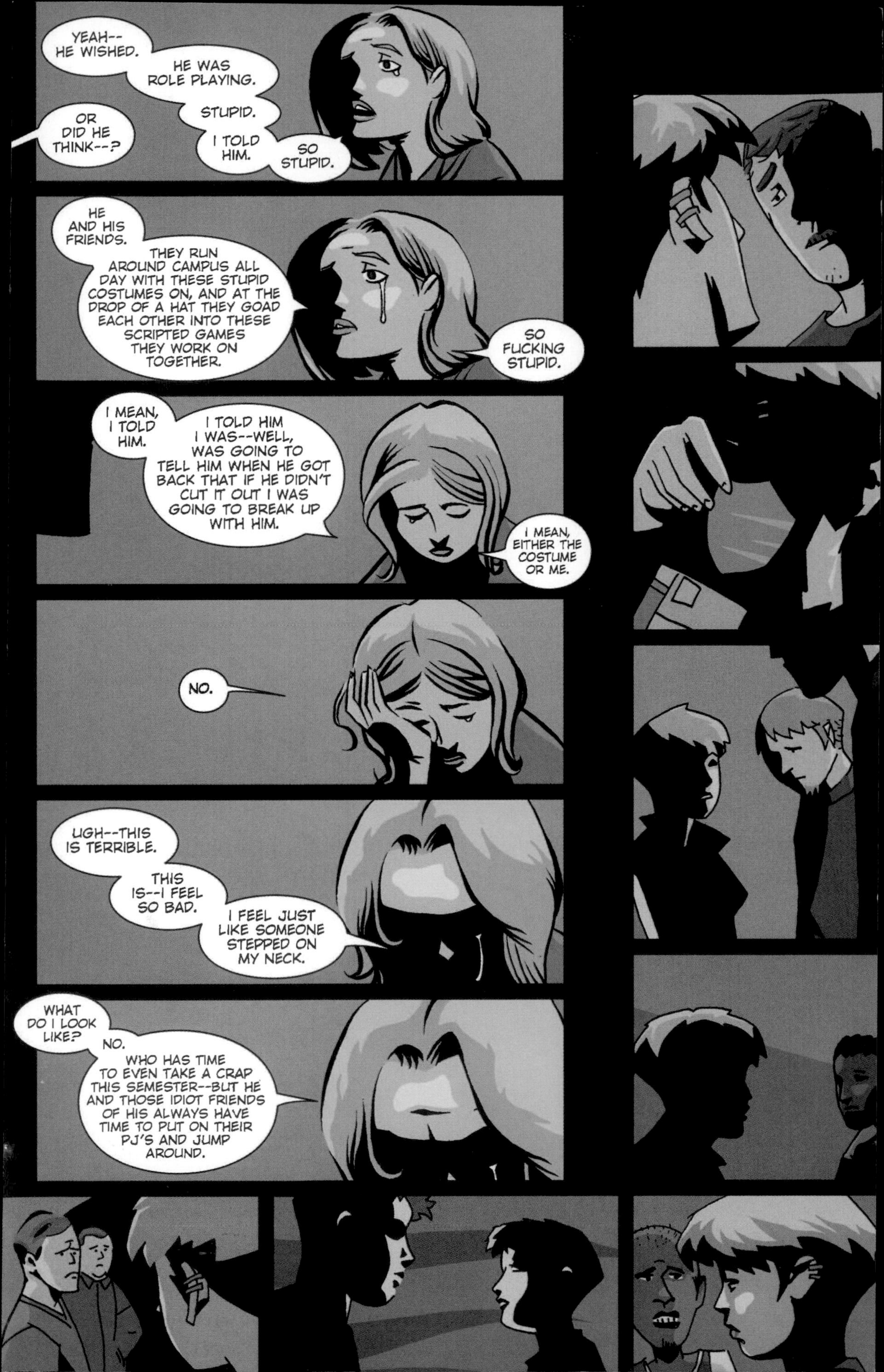
YEAH-- HE WISHED.
HE WAS ROLE PLAYING.
STUPID.
I TOLD HIM.
SO STUPID.
OR DID HE THINK--?
HE AND HIS FRIENDS.
THEY RUN AROUND CAMPUS ALL DAY WITH THESE STUPID COSTUMES ON, AND AT THE DROP OF A HAT THEY GOAD EACH OTHER INTO THESE SCRIPTED GAMES THEY WORK ON TOGETHER.
SO FUCKING STUPID.
I MEAN, I TOLD HIM.
I TOLD HIM I WAS--WELL, WAS GOING TO TELL HIM WHEN HE GOT BACK THAT IF HE DIDN'T CUT IT OUT I WAS GOING TO BREAK UP WITH HIM.
I MEAN, EITHER THE COSTUME OR ME.
NO.
UGH--THIS IS TERRIBLE.
THIS IS--I FEEL SO BAD.
I FEEL JUST LIKE SOMEONE STEPPED ON MY NECK.
WHAT DO I LOOK LIKE?
NO.
WHO HAS TIME TO EVEN TAKE A CRAP THIS SEMESTER--BUT HE AND THOSE IDIOT FRIENDS OF HIS ALWAYS HAVE TIME TO PUT ON THEIR PJ'S AND JUMP AROUND.

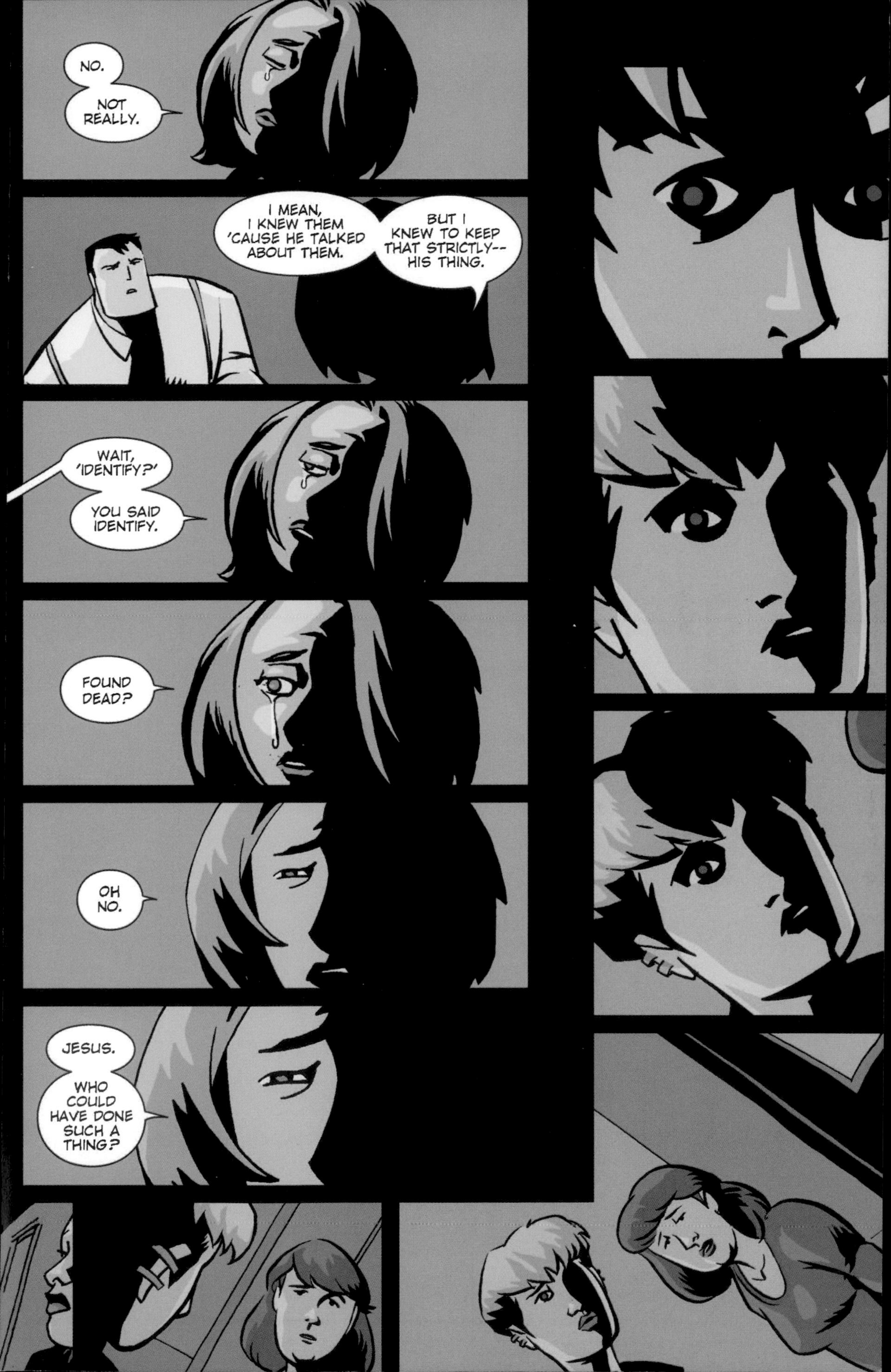
NO.
NOT REALLY.
I MEAN, I KNEW THEM 'CAUSE HE TALKED ABOUT THEM.
BUT I KNEW TO KEEP THAT STRICTLY-- HIS THING.
WAIT, 'IDENTIFY?'
YOU SAID IDENTIFY.
FOUND DEAD?
OH NO.
JESUS.
WHO COULD HAVE DONE SUCH A THING?

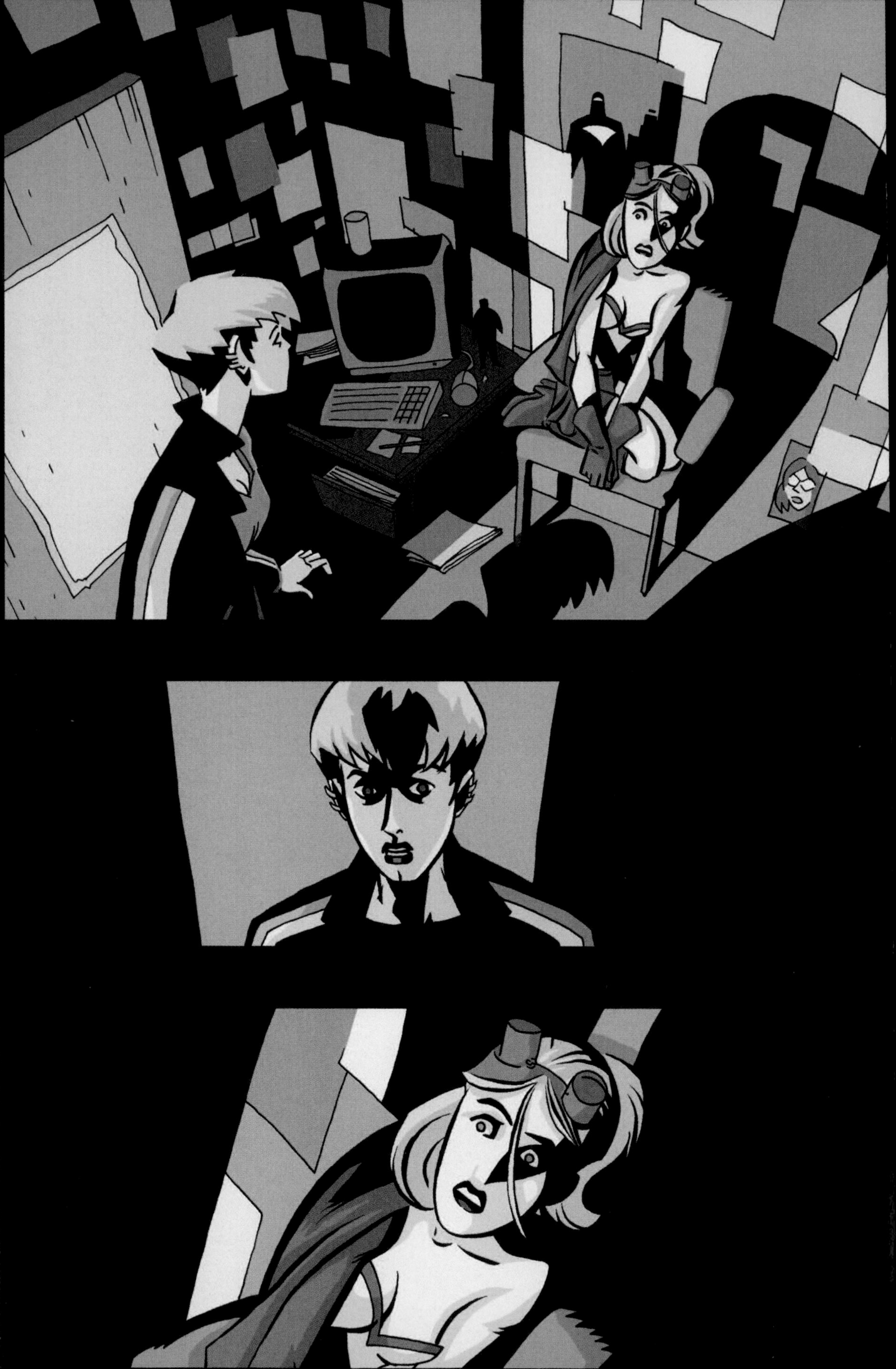

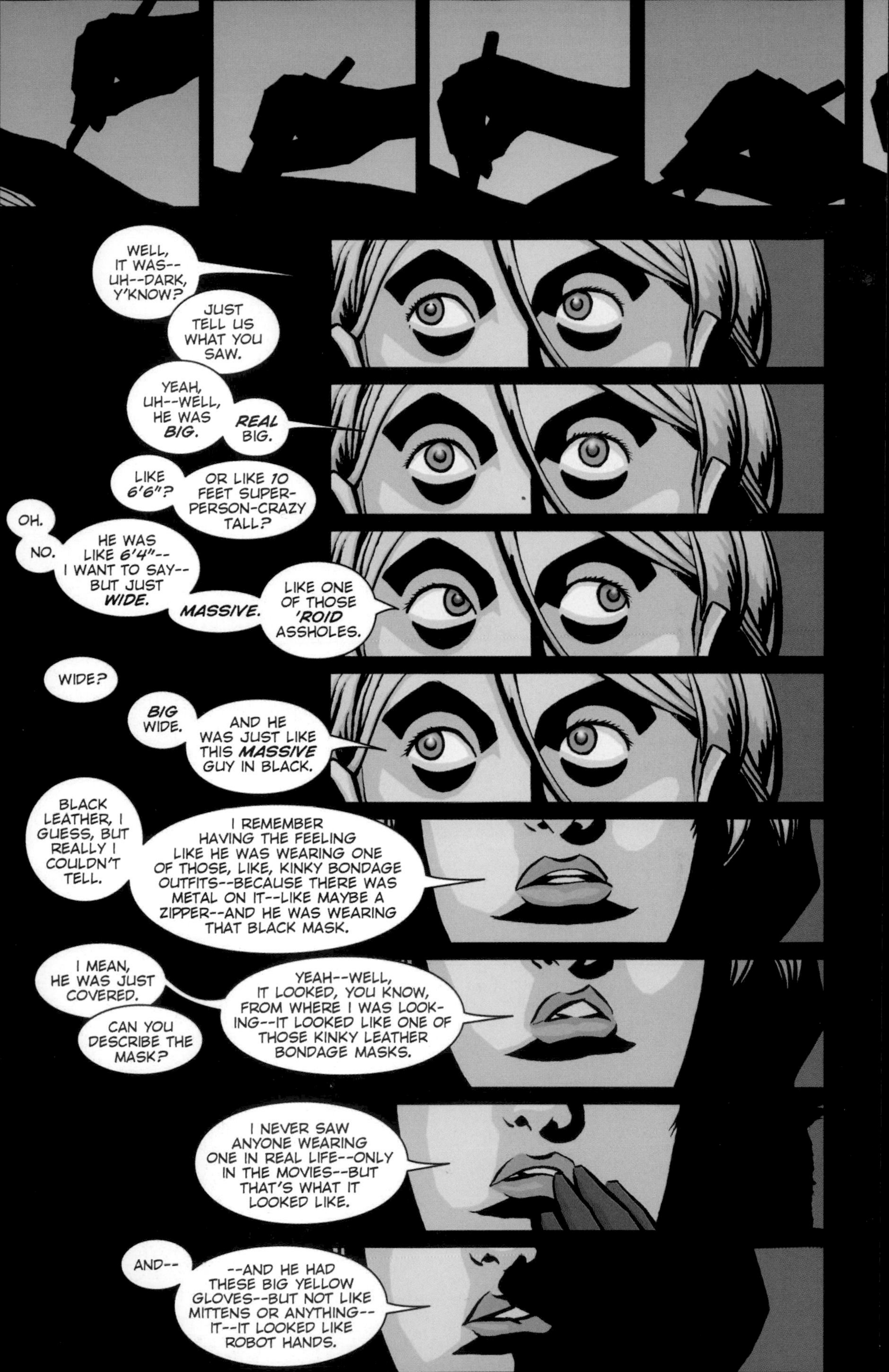
WELL, IT WAS--UH--DARK, Y'KNOW?
JUST TELL US WHAT YOU SAW.
YEAH, UH--WELL, HE WAS BIG.
REAL BIG.
LIKE 6'6"?
OR LIKE 10 FEET SUPER-PERSON-CRAZY TALL?
OH.
NO.
HE WAS LIKE 6'4"-- I WANT TO SAY-- BUT JUST WIDE.
MASSIVE.
LIKE ONE OF THOSE 'ROID ASSHOLES.
WIDE?
BIG WIDE.
AND HE WAS JUST LIKE THIS MASSIVE GUY IN BLACK.
BLACK LEATHER, I GUESS, BUT REALLY I COULDN'T TELL.
I REMEMBER HAVING THE FEELING LIKE HE WAS WEARING ONE OF THOSE, LIKE, KINKY BONDAGE OUTFITS--BECAUSE THERE WAS METAL ON IT--LIKE MAYBE A ZIPPER--AND HE WAS WEARING THAT BLACK MASK.
I MEAN, HE WAS JUST COVERED.
CAN YOU DESCRIBE THE MASK?
YEAH--WELL, IT LOOKED, YOU KNOW, FROM WHERE I WAS LOOK-ING--IT LOOKED LIKE ONE OF THOSE KINKY LEATHER BONDAGE MASKS.
I NEVER SAW ANYONE WEARING ONE IN REAL LIFE--ONLY IN THE MOVIES--BUT THAT'S WHAT IT LOOKED LIKE.
AND--
--AND HE HAD THESE BIG YELLOW GLOVES--BUT NOT LIKE MITTENS OR ANYTHING--IT--IT LOOKED LIKE ROBOT HANDS.

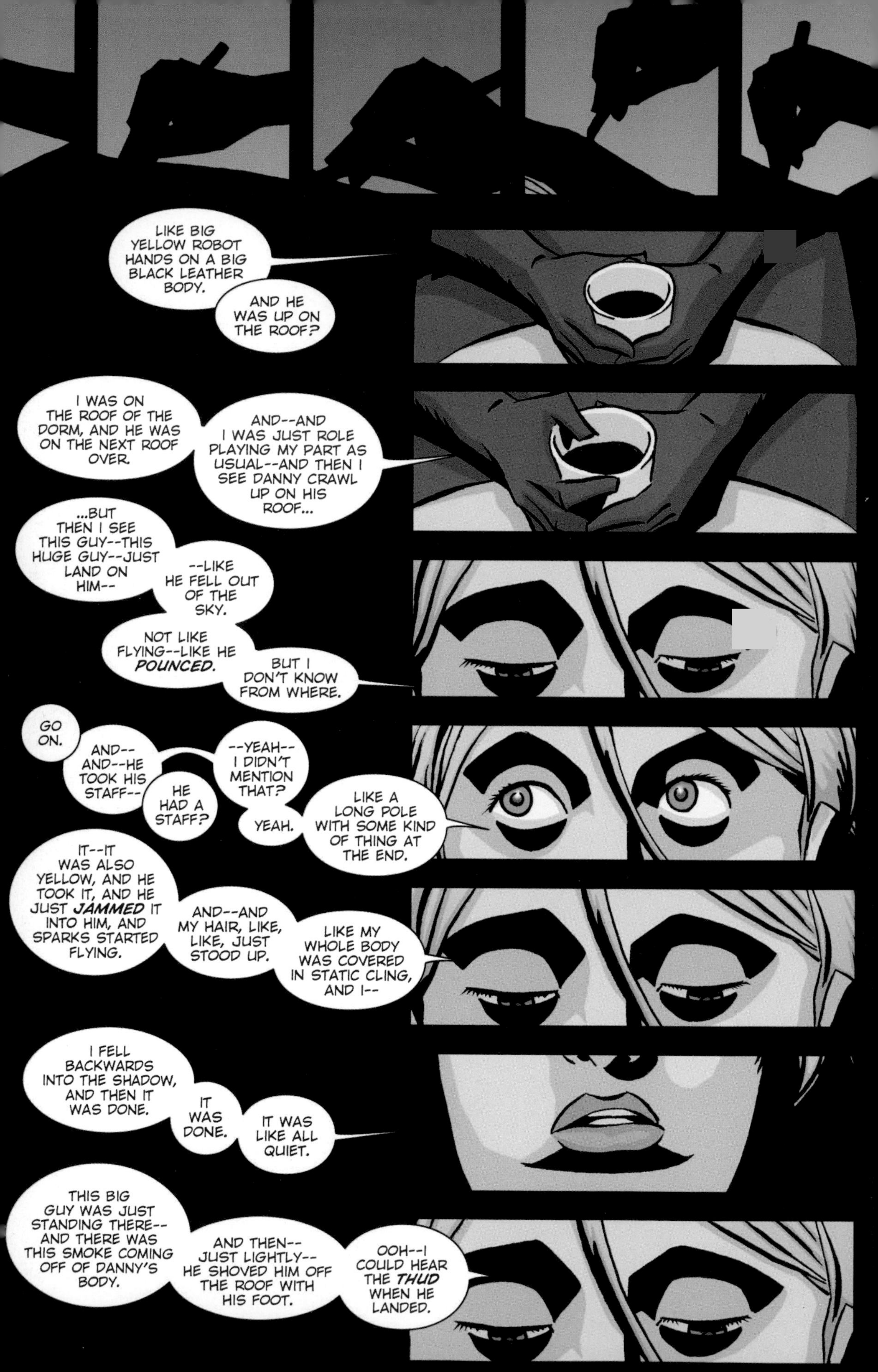

LIKE BIG YELLOW ROBOT HANDS ON A BIG BLACK LEATHER BODY.
AND HE WAS UP ON THE ROOF?
I WAS ON THE ROOF OF THE DORM, AND HE WAS ON THE NEXT ROOF OVER.
AND--AND I WAS JUST ROLE PLAYING MY PART AS USUAL--AND THEN I SEE DANNY CRAWL UP ON HIS ROOF...
...BUT THEN I SEE THIS GUY--THIS HUGE GUY--JUST LAND ON HIM--
--LIKE HE FELL OUT OF THE SKY.
NOT LIKE FLYING--LIKE HE *POUNCED.*
BUT I DON'T KNOW FROM WHERE.
GO ON.
AND--AND--HE TOOK HIS STAFF--
HE HAD A STAFF?
--YEAH--I DIDN'T MENTION THAT?
YEAH.
LIKE A LONG POLE WITH SOME KIND OF THING AT THE END.
IT--IT WAS ALSO YELLOW, AND HE TOOK IT, AND HE JUST *JAMMED* IT INTO HIM, AND SPARKS STARTED FLYING.
AND--AND MY HAIR, LIKE, LIKE, JUST STOOD UP.
LIKE MY WHOLE BODY WAS COVERED IN STATIC CLING, AND I--
I FELL BACKWARDS INTO THE SHADOW, AND THEN IT WAS DONE.
IT WAS DONE.
IT WAS LIKE ALL QUIET.
THIS BIG GUY WAS JUST STANDING THERE--AND THERE WAS THIS SMOKE COMING OFF OF DANNY'S BODY.
AND THEN--JUST LIGHTLY--HE SHOVED HIM OFF THE ROOF WITH HIS FOOT.
OOH--I COULD HEAR THE *THUD* WHEN HE LANDED.

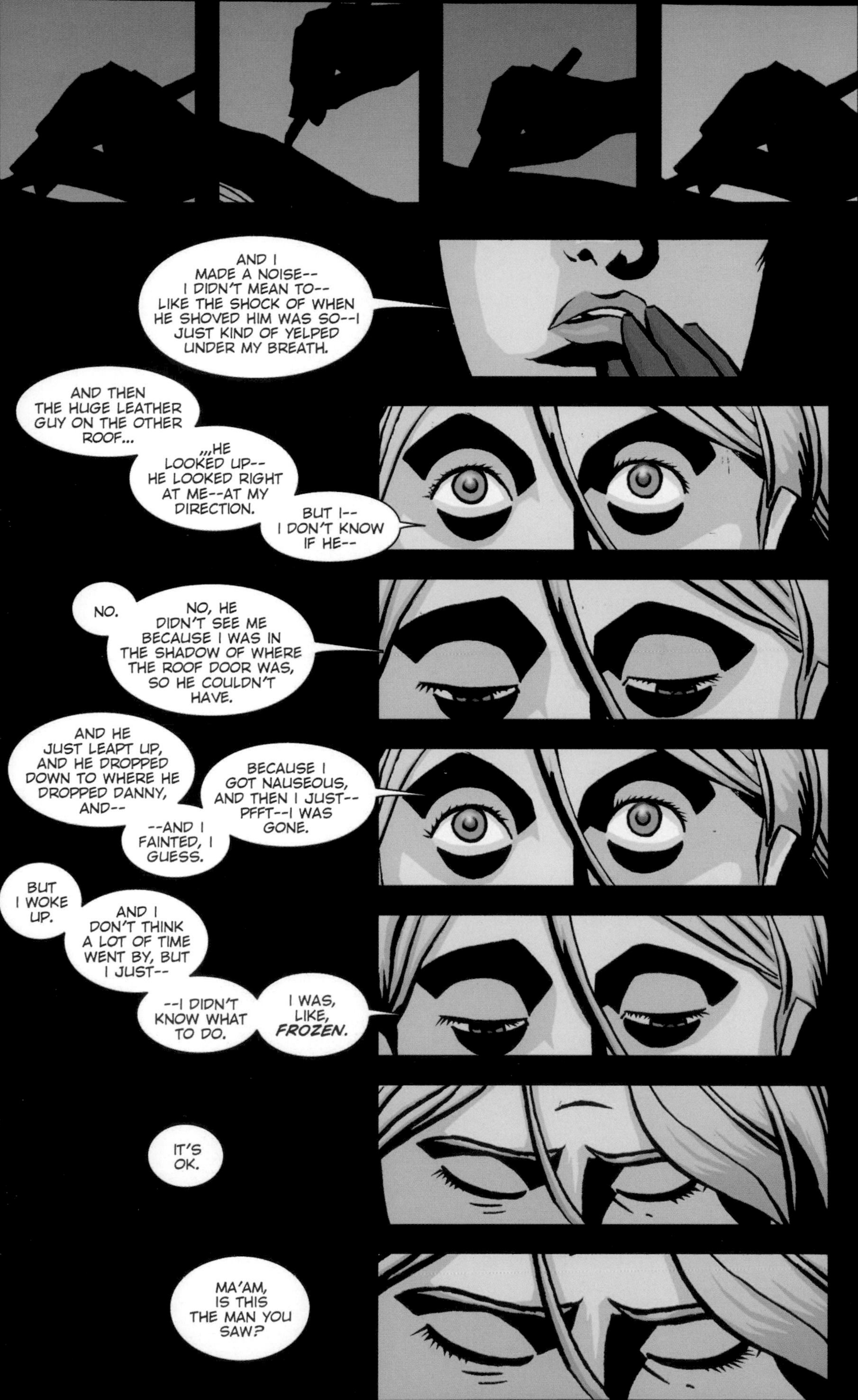
AND I MADE A NOISE-- I DIDN'T MEAN TO-- LIKE THE SHOCK OF WHEN HE SHOVED HIM WAS SO--I JUST KIND OF YELPED UNDER MY BREATH.
AND THEN THE HUGE LEATHER GUY ON THE OTHER ROOF...
...HE LOOKED UP-- HE LOOKED RIGHT AT ME--AT MY DIRECTION.
BUT I-- I DON'T KNOW IF HE--
NO.
NO, HE DIDN'T SEE ME BECAUSE I WAS IN THE SHADOW OF WHERE THE ROOF DOOR WAS, SO HE COULDN'T HAVE.
AND HE JUST LEAPT UP, AND HE DROPPED DOWN TO WHERE HE DROPPED DANNY, AND--
--AND I FAINTED, I GUESS.
BECAUSE I GOT NAUSEOUS, AND THEN I JUST-- PFFT--I WAS GONE.
BUT I WOKE UP.
AND I DON'T THINK A LOT OF TIME WENT BY, BUT I JUST--
--I DIDN'T KNOW WHAT TO DO.
I WAS, LIKE, *FROZEN*.
IT'S OK.
MA'AM, IS THIS THE MAN YOU SAW?

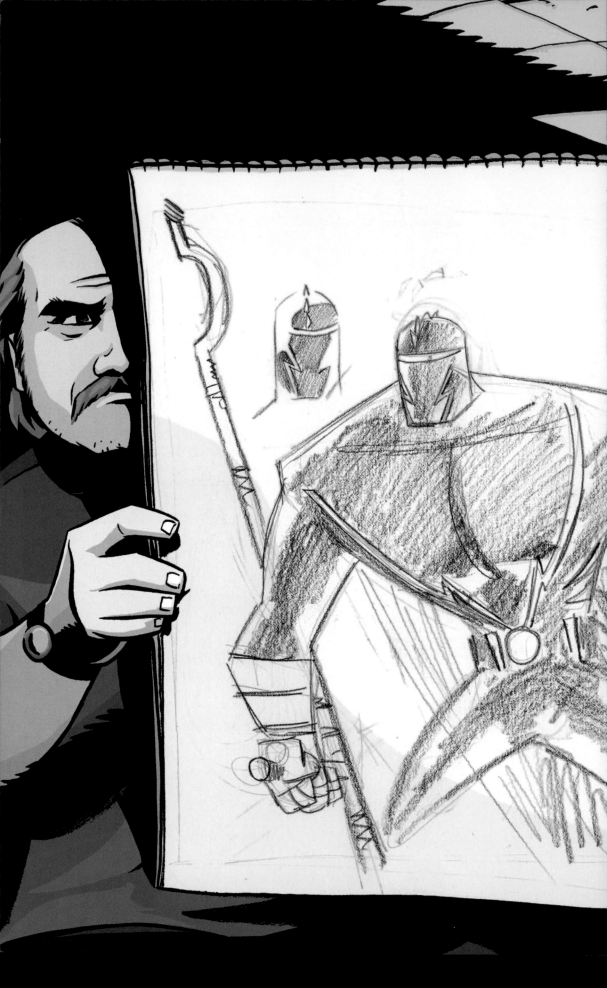

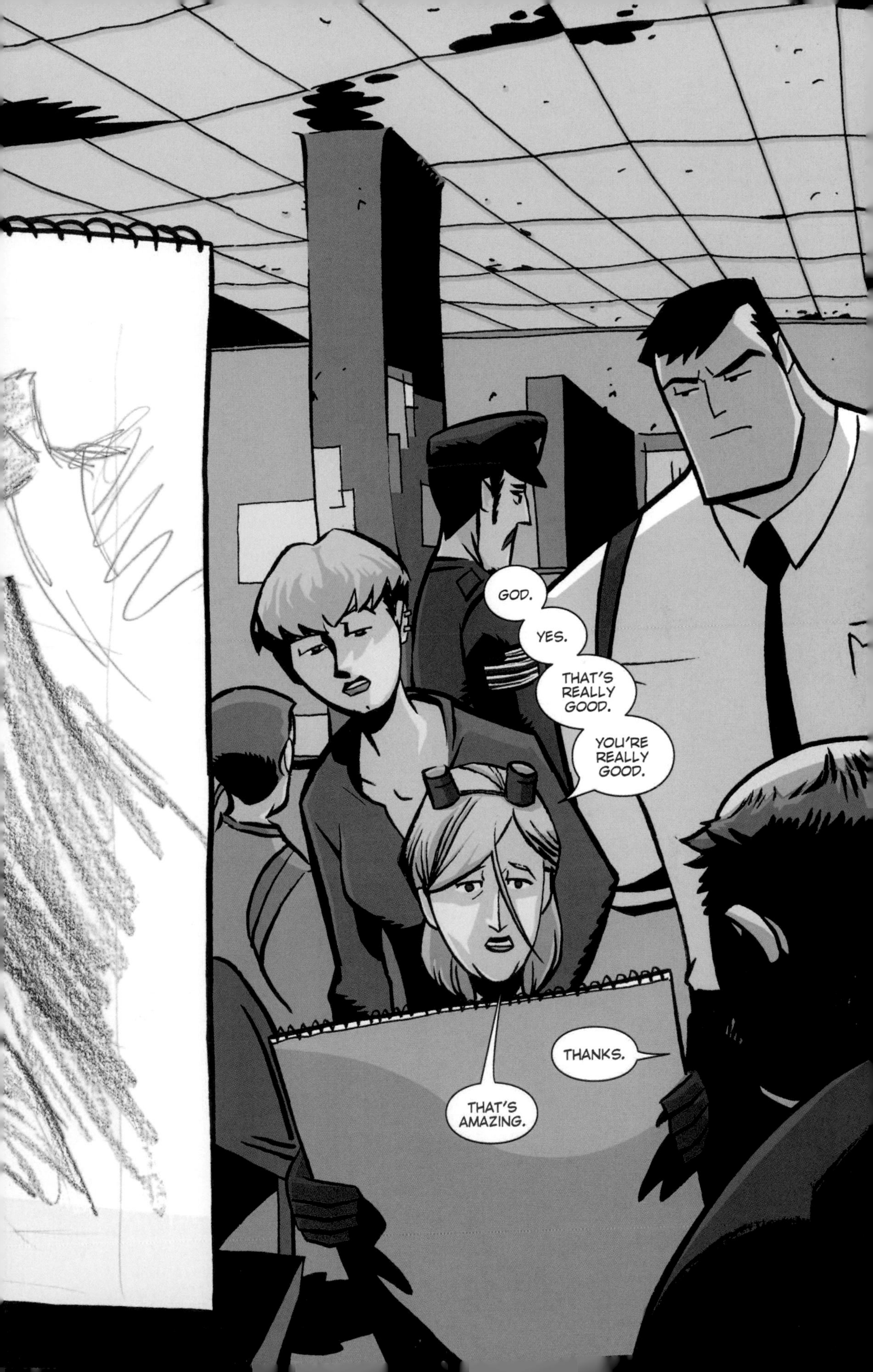
GOD.
YES.
THAT'S REALLY GOOD.
YOU'RE REALLY GOOD.
THAT'S AMAZING.
THANKS.

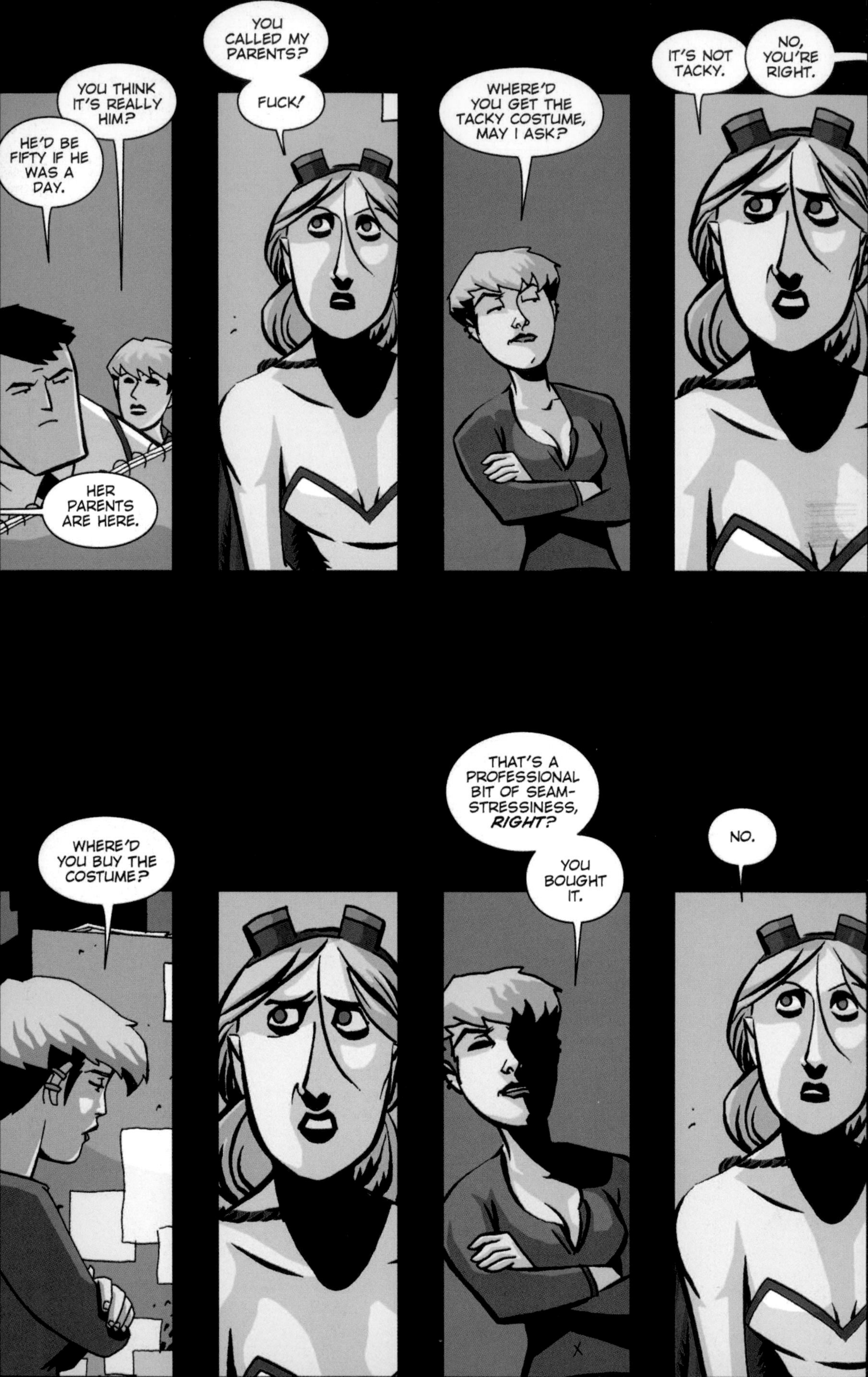
HE'D BE FIFTY IF HE WAS A DAY.
YOU THINK IT'S REALLY HIM?
HER PARENTS ARE HERE.
YOU CALLED MY PARENTS?
FUCK!
WHERE'D YOU GET THE TACKY COSTUME, MAY I ASK?
IT'S NOT TACKY.
NO, YOU'RE RIGHT.
WHERE'D YOU BUY THE COSTUME?
THAT'S A PROFESSIONAL BIT OF SEAM-STRESSINESS, RIGHT?
YOU BOUGHT IT.
NO.

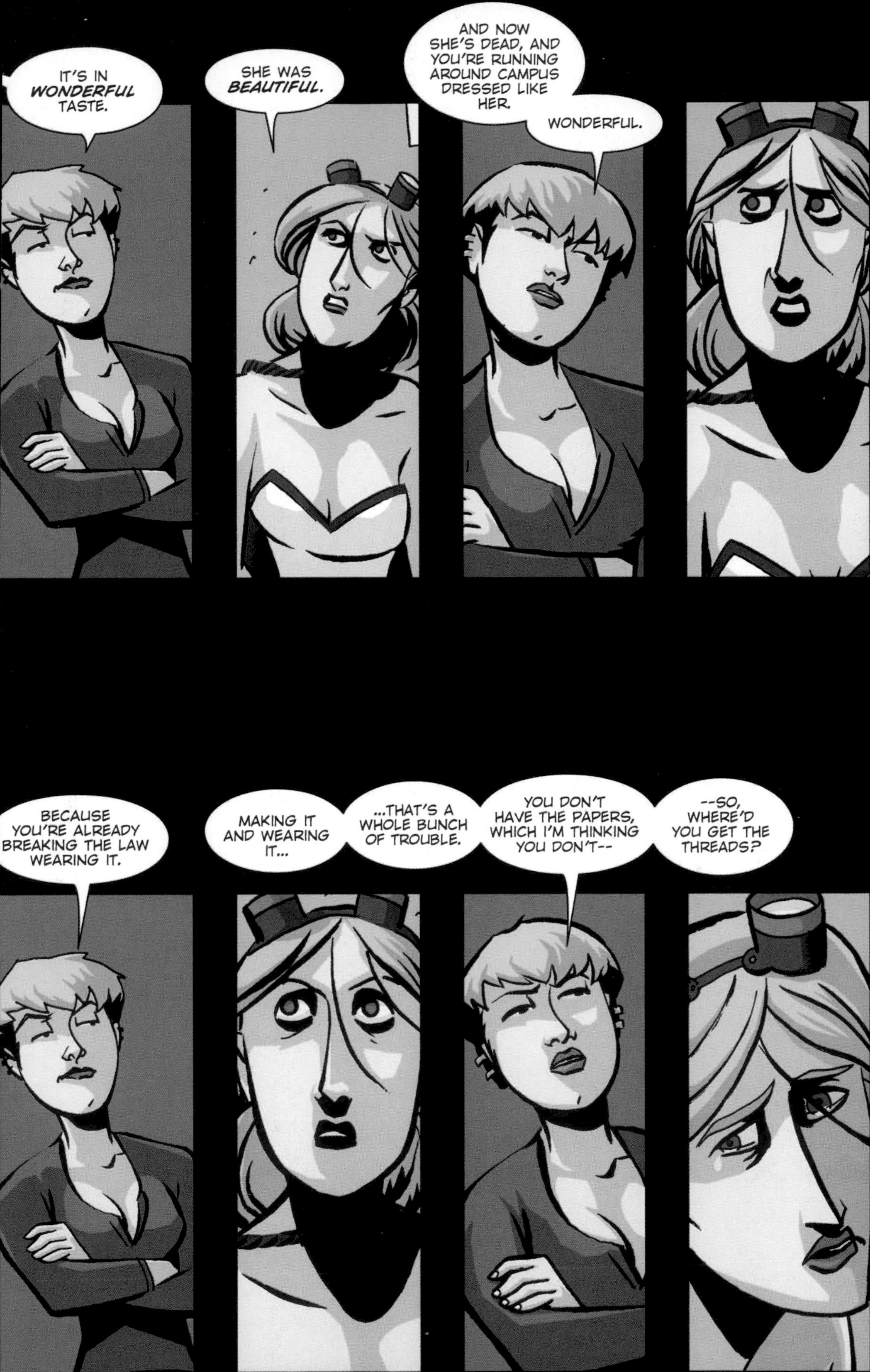
IT'S IN *WONDERFUL* TASTE.
SHE WAS *BEAUTIFUL.*
AND NOW SHE'S DEAD, AND YOU'RE RUNNING AROUND CAMPUS DRESSED LIKE HER.
WONDERFUL.
BECAUSE YOU'RE ALREADY BREAKING THE LAW WEARING IT.
MAKING IT AND WEARING IT...
...THAT'S A WHOLE BUNCH OF TROUBLE.
YOU DON'T HAVE THE PAPERS, WHICH I'M THINKING YOU DON'T--
--SO, WHERE'D YOU GET THE THREADS?

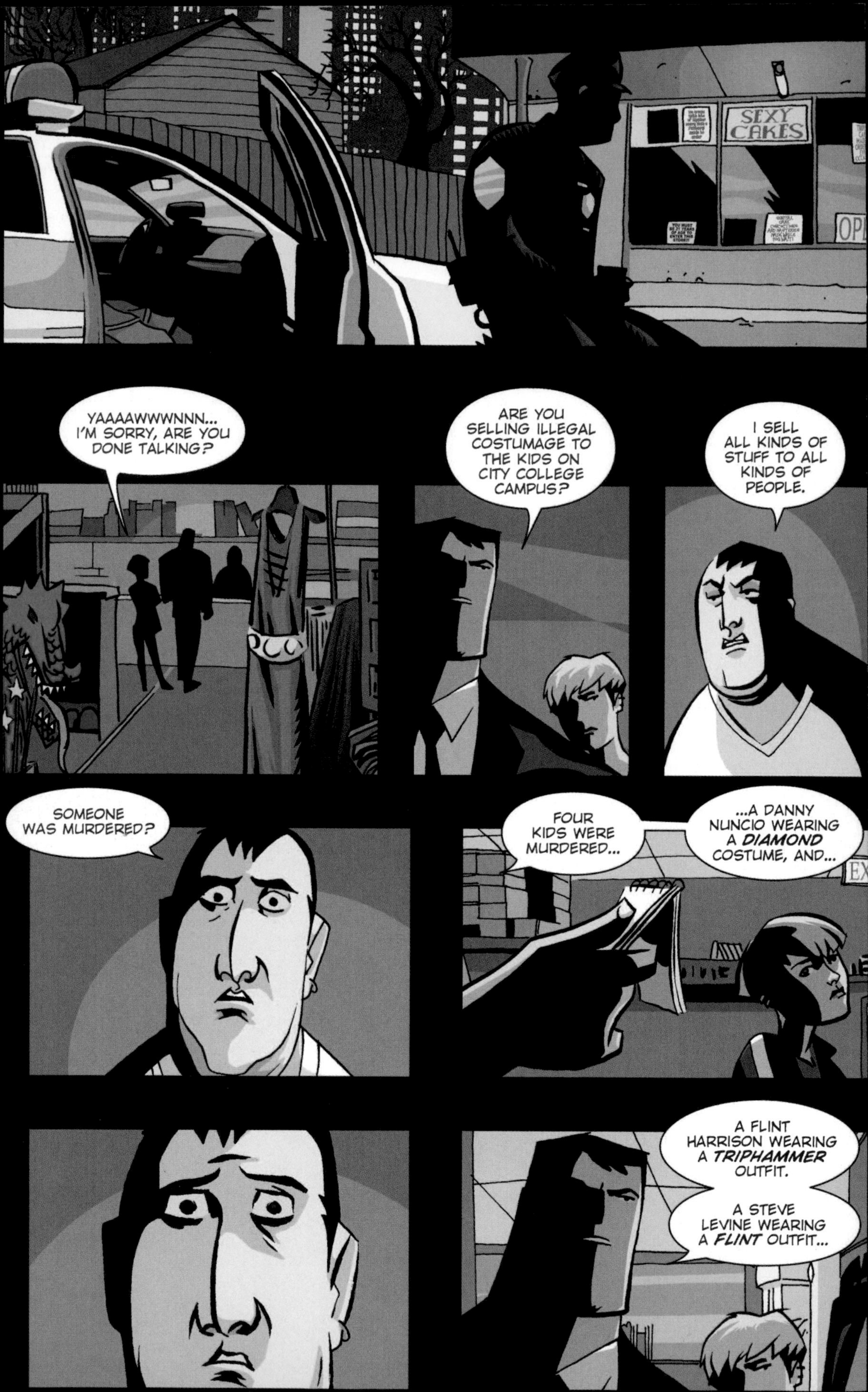
SEXY CAKES
YAAAAWWWNNN... I'M SORRY, ARE YOU DONE TALKING?
ARE YOU SELLING ILLEGAL COSTUMAGE TO THE KIDS ON CITY COLLEGE CAMPUS?
I SELL ALL KINDS OF STUFF TO ALL KINDS OF PEOPLE.
SOMEONE WAS MURDERED?
FOUR KIDS WERE MURDERED...
...A DANNY NUNCIO WEARING A ***DIAMOND*** COSTUME, AND...
A FLINT HARRISON WEARING A ***TRIPHAMMER*** OUTFIT.
A STEVE LEVINE WEARING A ***FLINT*** OUTFIT...

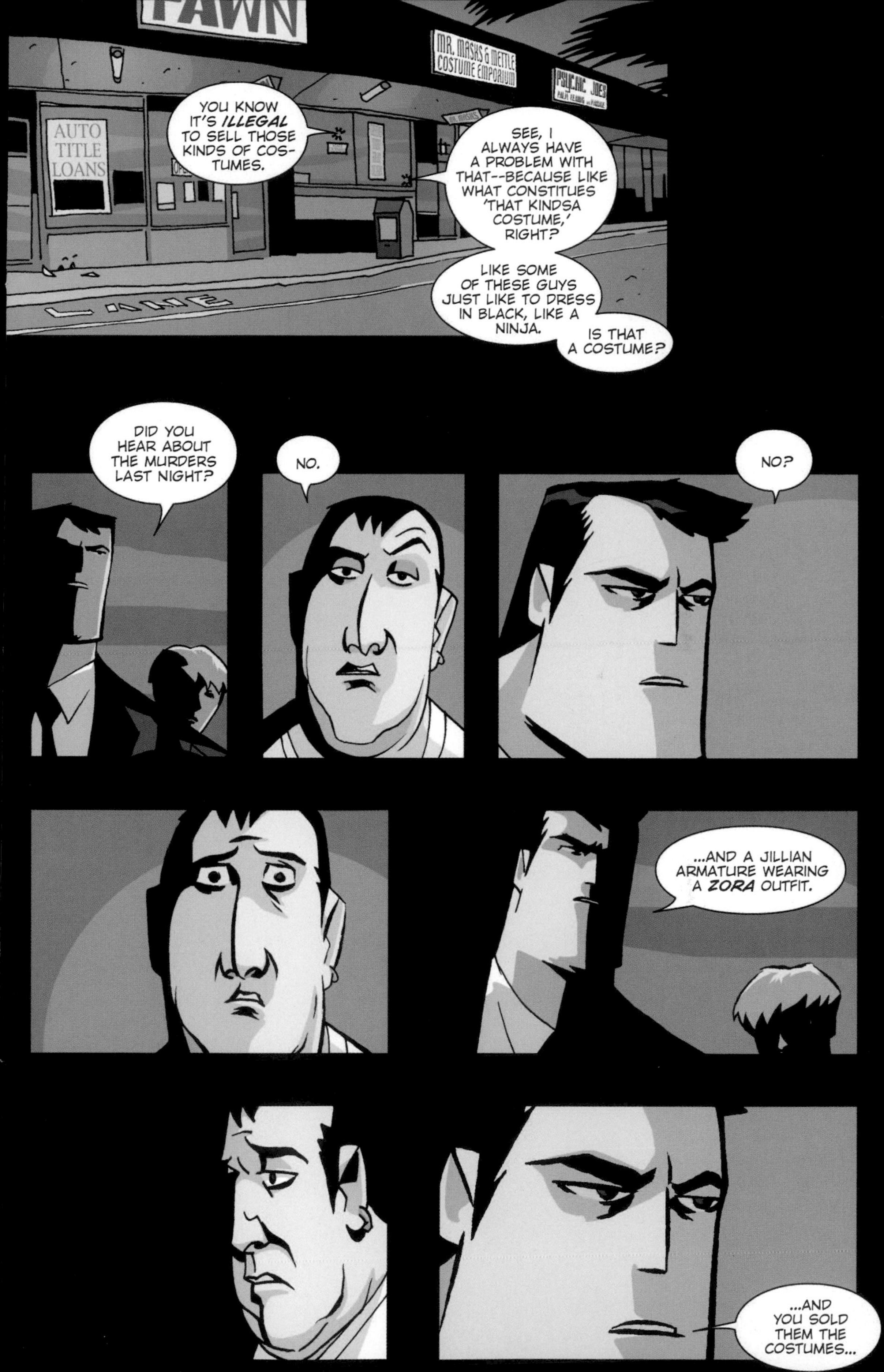
PAWN
MR. MASKS & METTLE COSTUME EMPORIUM
PSYCHIC JOES
AUTO TITLE LOANS
LANE
YOU KNOW IT'S *ILLEGAL* TO SELL THOSE KINDS OF COS-TUMES.
SEE, I ALWAYS HAVE A PROBLEM WITH THAT--BECAUSE LIKE WHAT CONSTITUES 'THAT KINDSA COSTUME,' RIGHT?
LIKE SOME OF THESE GUYS JUST LIKE TO DRESS IN BLACK, LIKE A NINJA.
IS THAT A COSTUME?
DID YOU HEAR ABOUT THE MURDERS LAST NIGHT?
NO.
NO?
...AND A JILLIAN ARMATURE WEARING A *ZORA* OUTFIT.
...AND YOU SOLD THEM THE COSTUMES...

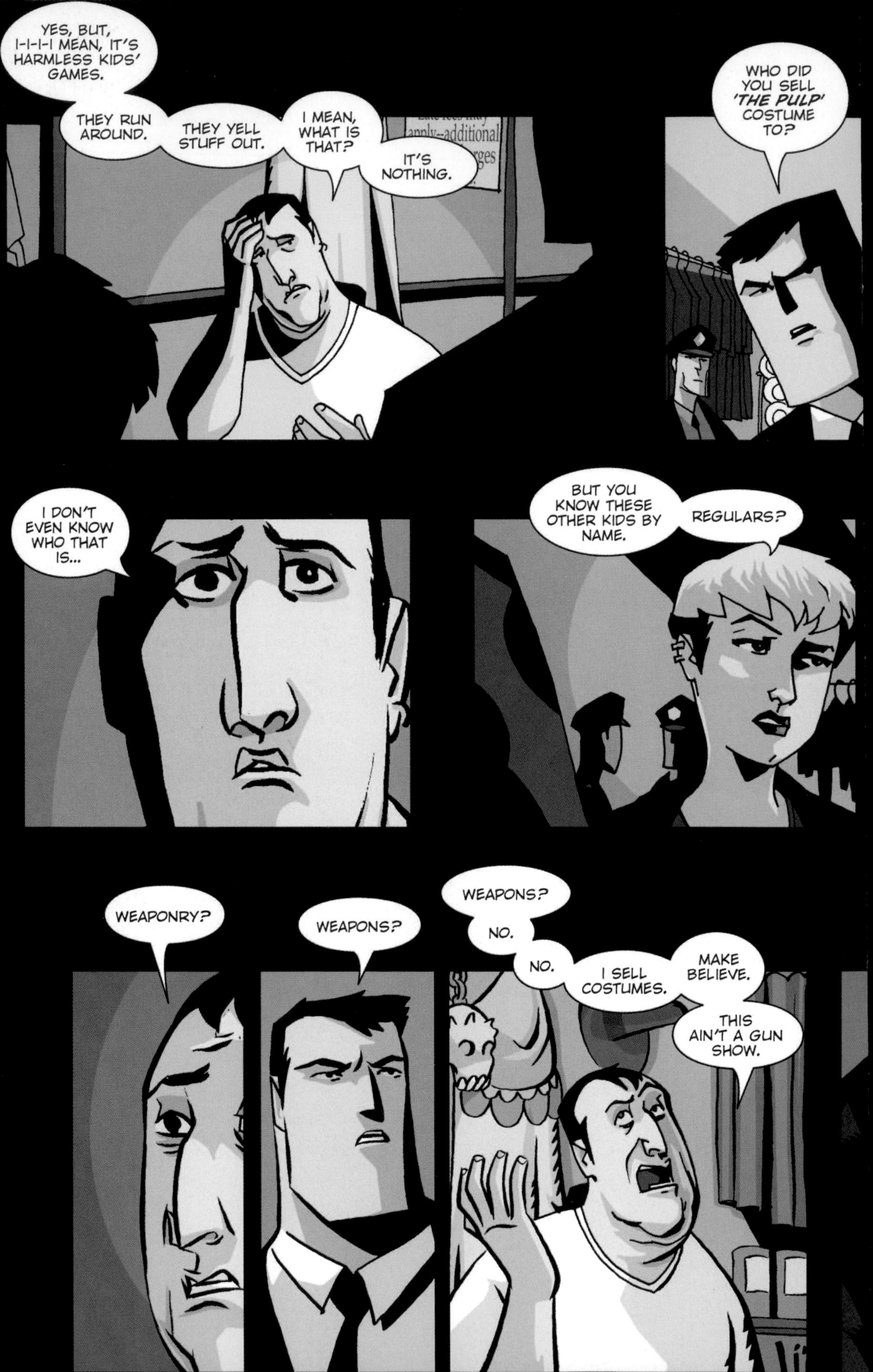
YES, BUT, I-I-I-I MEAN, IT'S HARMLESS KIDS' GAMES.
THEY RUN AROUND.
THEY YELL STUFF OUT.
I MEAN, WHAT IS THAT?
IT'S NOTHING.
WHO DID YOU SELL *'THE PULP'* COSTUME TO?
I DON'T EVEN KNOW WHO THAT IS...
BUT YOU KNOW THESE OTHER KIDS BY NAME.
REGULARS?
WEAPONRY?
WEAPONS?
WEAPONS?
NO.
NO.
I SELL COSTUMES.
MAKE BELIEVE.
THIS AIN'T A GUN SHOW.

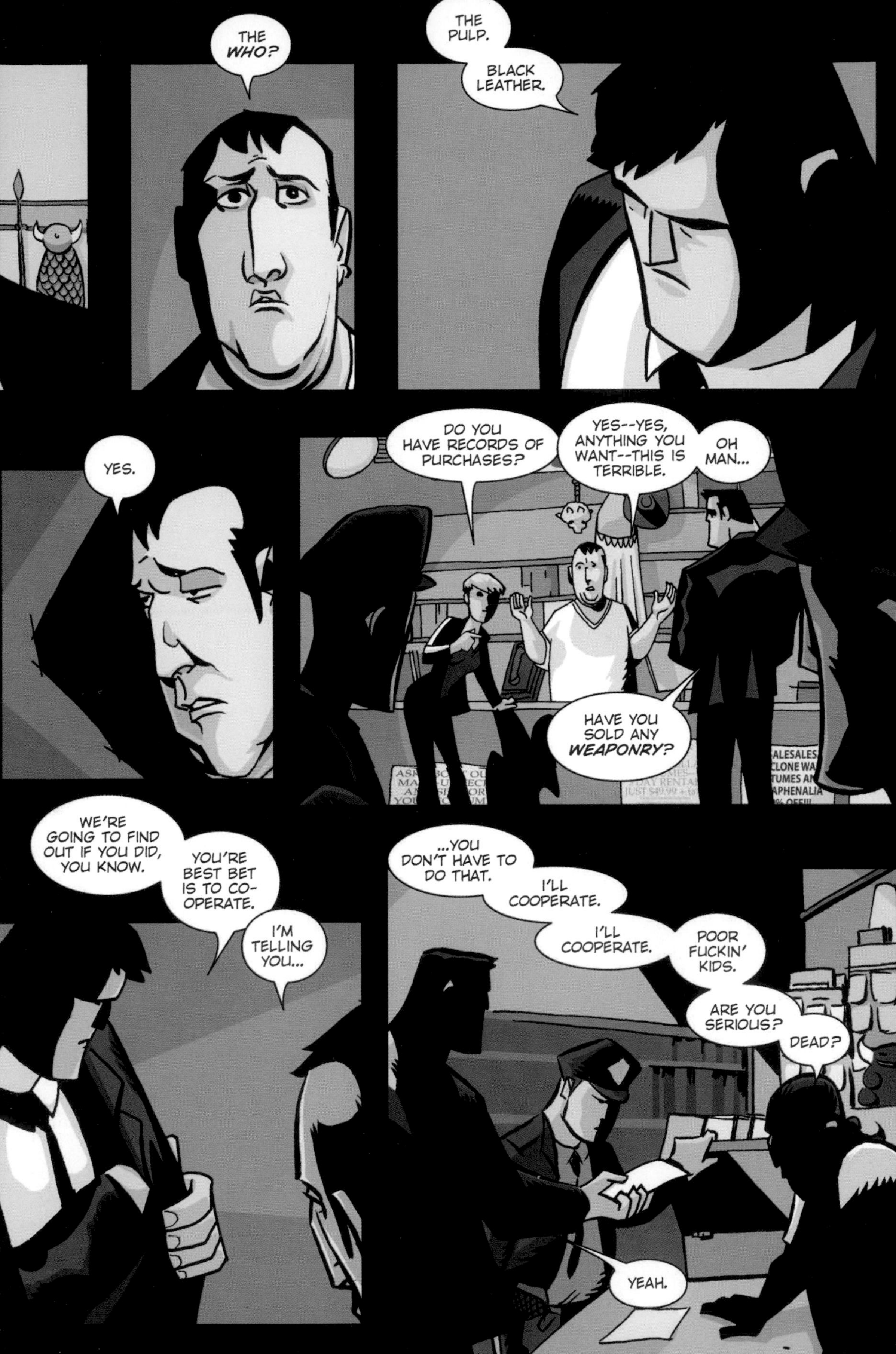
THE WHO?
THE PULP.
BLACK LEATHER.
YES.
DO YOU HAVE RECORDS OF PURCHASES?
YES--YES, ANYTHING YOU WANT--THIS IS TERRIBLE.
OH MAN...
HAVE YOU SOLD ANY WEAPONRY?
WE'RE GOING TO FIND OUT IF YOU DID, YOU KNOW.
YOU'RE BEST BET IS TO CO-OPERATE.
I'M TELLING YOU...
...YOU DON'T HAVE TO DO THAT.
I'LL COOPERATE.
I'LL COOPERATE.
POOR FUCKIN' KIDS.
ARE YOU SERIOUS?
DEAD?
YEAH.

NOT MUCH FOOTAGE EXISTS OF THE NOTORIOUS *PULP*.

LIKE MANY OF THE SHADOWY FIGURES THAT HAVE INHABIT-ED THE CITY OVER THE YEARS, THE *PULP* HAS KEPT A DECIDEDLY LOW PROFILE.

FOR MANY YEARS HE WAS CONSIDERED THE STUFF OF ORGANIZED CRIME FOLKLORE.

A NAME THAT SMALL-TIME HOODS GAVE THE POLICE TO THROW THEM OFF THEIR TRAIL.

BUT TONIGHT ON *'POWER CORRUPTS'*, WE WILL EXPLORE THROUGH *EXCLUSIVE* INTERVIEWS AND NEWLY SURFACED INFORMA-TION, SOME OF THE FACTS BEHIND THE MYTH.

OK. ALRIGHT--SO THERE'S TWO KINDS OF GUYS WITH POWERS-- THE GUYS THAT HAD POWERS GIVEN TO THEM BY, YOU KNOW, BIRTHRIGHT, ACCIDENT--AND THEN THERE'S THE GUYS WHO GO LOOKING TO GET POWERS.

AND I TELL YA, THESE ARE THE GUYS THAT SCARE YA. THEY ARE THE TROUBLE TOMMYS. MICROBES, WE CALL THEM. EVERY TIME ONE O' THESE GUYS, LIKE, SCIENTI-FICALLY FINDS A WAY TO GET POWERS... WHAT HAPPENS? THEY UNHINGE. LIKE 'ROID RAGE.

THEY THINK THAT THEY'RE, LIKE, THE NEXT STEP OF HUMAN EVOLU-TION. THINK THEY'RE MORE THAN HUMAN, WHICH OF COURSE AIN'T THE TRUTH. NO. SEE, THEY SORTA MADE THEMSELVES INTO SOMETHING, LIKE, A LOT LESS THAN HUMAN.

BUT TRY TELLING THEM THAT. SEE WHAT HAPPENS...

...AND YEAH, SURE--I SEEN THE PULP ONCE.

MET THE CREEPY BASTARD AS PART OF THIS THING.

WHAT KIND OF THING?
A THING. YOU KNOW...LET'S LEAVE IT AT THAT. AND AS SOON AS I SAW HIM--I SAID: MICROBE. YOU COULD SEE IT IN HIS EYE. HE WAS ALREADY HALF OUT THE DOOR, IF YOU KNOW WHAT I MEAN.

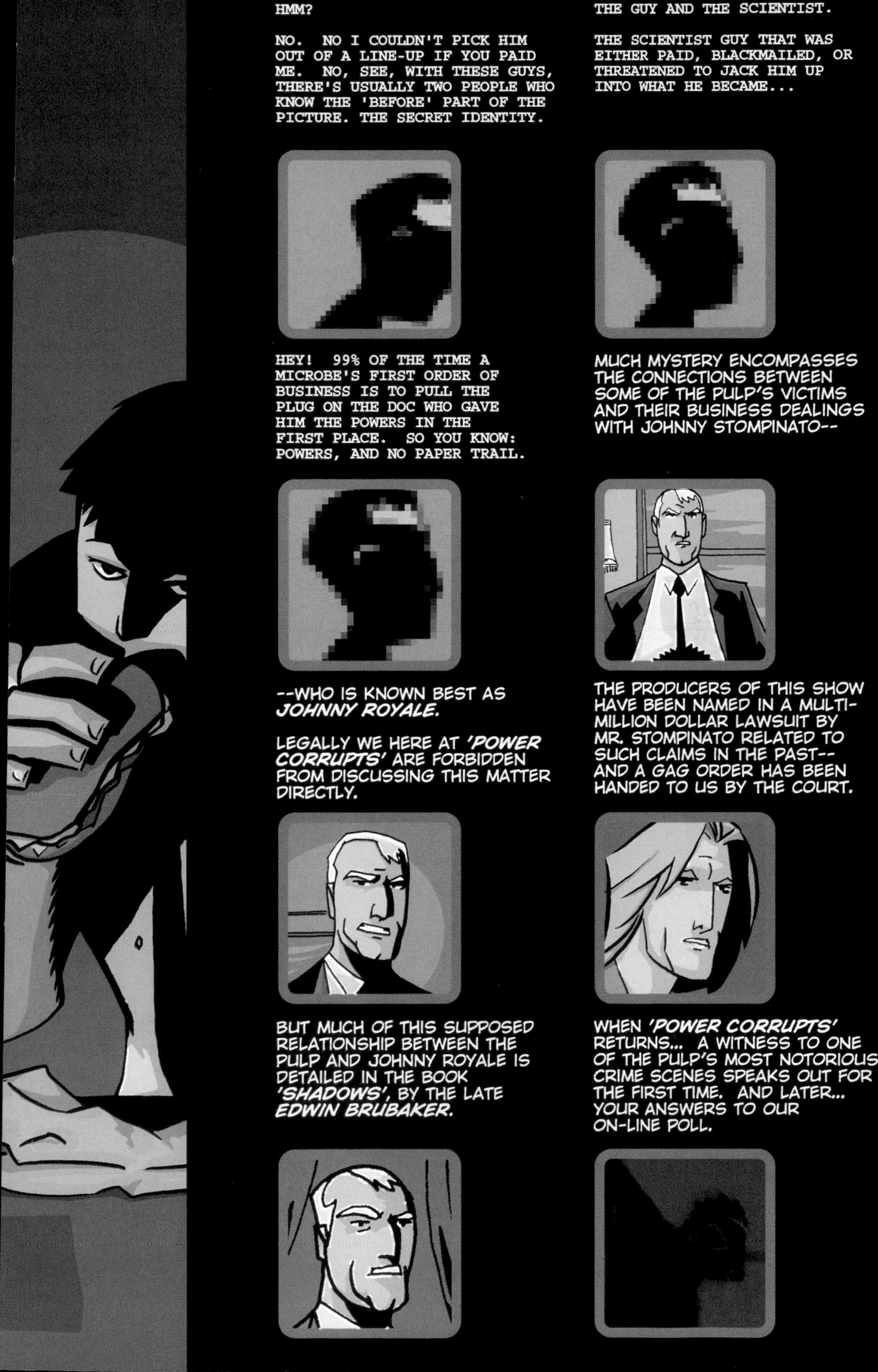
HMM?
NO. NO I COULDN'T PICK HIM OUT OF A LINE-UP IF YOU PAID ME. NO, SEE, WITH THESE GUYS, THERE'S USUALLY TWO PEOPLE WHO KNOW THE 'BEFORE' PART OF THE PICTURE. THE SECRET IDENTITY.
THE GUY AND THE SCIENTIST.
THE SCIENTIST GUY THAT WAS EITHER PAID, BLACKMAILED, OR THREATENED TO JACK HIM UP INTO WHAT HE BECAME...
HEY! 99% OF THE TIME A MICROBE'S FIRST ORDER OF BUSINESS IS TO PULL THE PLUG ON THE DOC WHO GAVE HIM THE POWERS IN THE FIRST PLACE. SO YOU KNOW: POWERS, AND NO PAPER TRAIL.
MUCH MYSTERY ENCOMPASSES THE CONNECTIONS BETWEEN SOME OF THE PULP'S VICTIMS AND THEIR BUSINESS DEALINGS WITH JOHNNY STOMPINATO--
--WHO IS KNOWN BEST AS *JOHNNY ROYALE.*
LEGALLY WE HERE AT *'POWER CORRUPTS'* ARE FORBIDDEN FROM DISCUSSING THIS MATTER DIRECTLY.
THE PRODUCERS OF THIS SHOW HAVE BEEN NAMED IN A MULTI-MILLION DOLLAR LAWSUIT BY MR. STOMPINATO RELATED TO SUCH CLAIMS IN THE PAST--AND A GAG ORDER HAS BEEN HANDED TO US BY THE COURT.
BUT MUCH OF THIS SUPPOSED RELATIONSHIP BETWEEN THE PULP AND JOHNNY ROYALE IS DETAILED IN THE BOOK *'SHADOWS'*, BY THE LATE *EDWIN BRUBAKER.*
WHEN *'POWER CORRUPTS'* RETURNS... A WITNESS TO ONE OF THE PULP'S MOST NOTORIOUS CRIME SCENES SPEAKS OUT FOR THE FIRST TIME. AND LATER... YOUR ANSWERS TO OUR ON-LINE POLL.

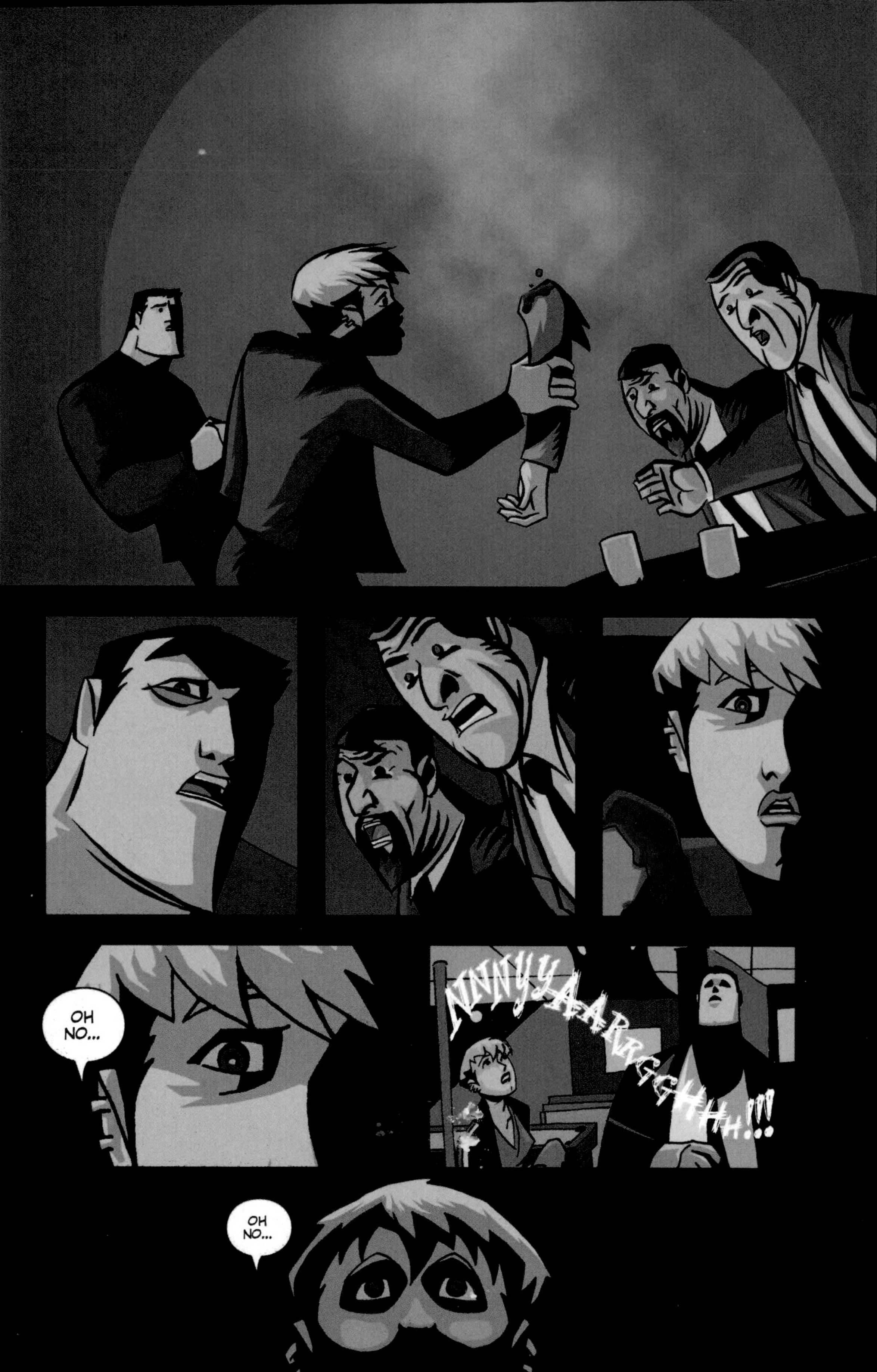
OH NO...
NNNYYAARRGGHHH!!!
OH NO...

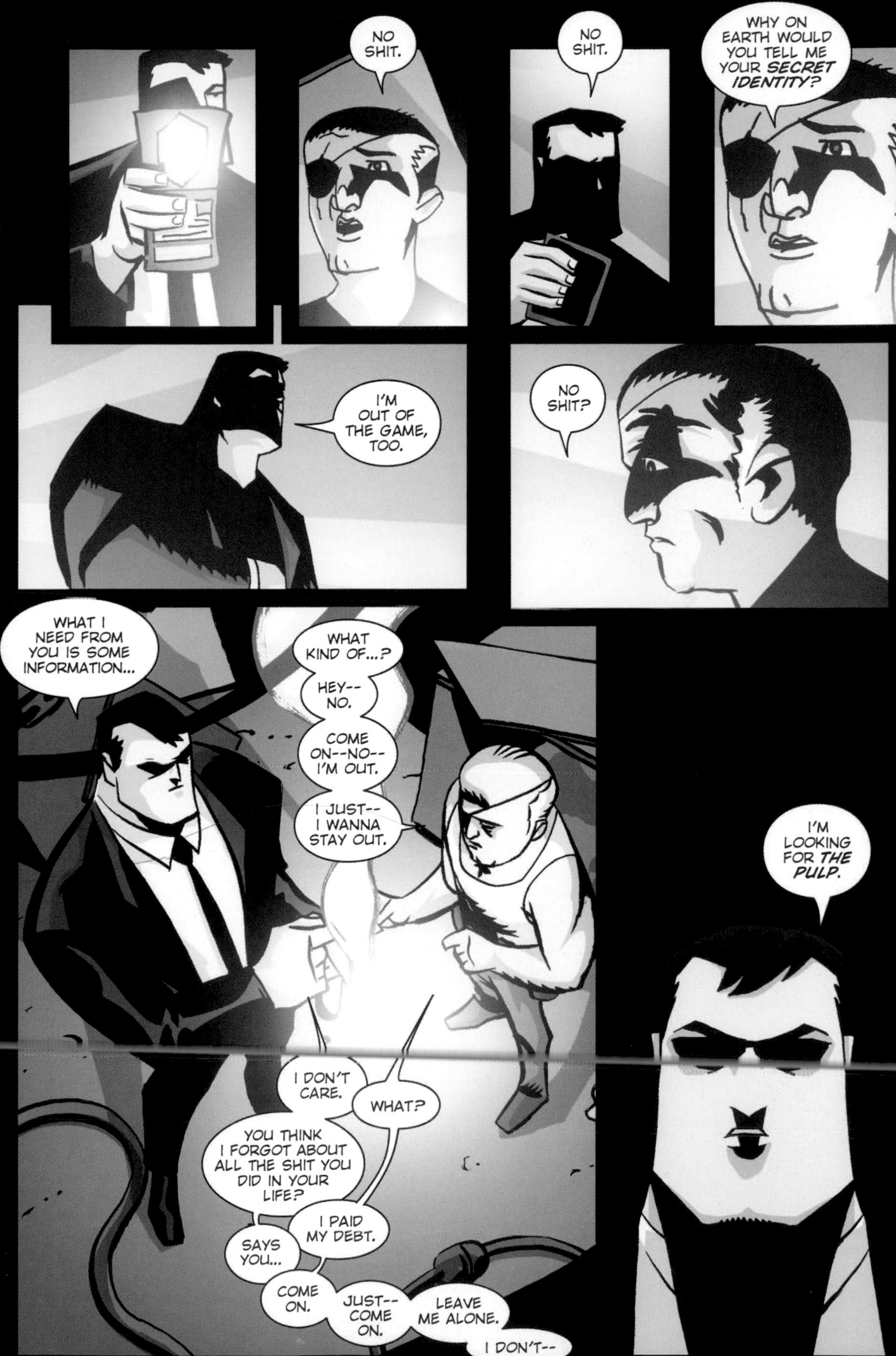
NO SHIT.
NO SHIT.
WHY ON EARTH WOULD YOU TELL ME YOUR SECRET IDENTITY?
I'M OUT OF THE GAME, TOO.
NO SHIT?
WHAT I NEED FROM YOU IS SOME INFORMATION...
WHAT KIND OF...?
HEY-- NO.
COME ON--NO-- I'M OUT.
I JUST-- I WANNA STAY OUT.
I'M LOOKING FOR THE PULP.
I DON'T CARE.
WHAT?
YOU THINK I FORGOT ABOUT ALL THE SHIT YOU DID IN YOUR LIFE?
I PAID MY DEBT.
SAYS YOU...
COME ON.
JUST-- COME ON.
LEAVE ME ALONE.
I DON'T--

HOTEL RULES:

1) NO COOKING--no hotplates or microwaves.
2) NO PETS.
3) NO VISITORS AFTER 8:00 P
4) NO DRUGS.
5) GUESTS/RESIDENTS MUST PAY IN ADVANCE.
6) NO SMOKING IN PUBLIC AREAS.
7) YOU BREAK IT, YOU BOUGH IT--you will be held accounta for all and any damages.
8) FRONT DOORS ARE LOCKE AT 9:00PM SHARP.
9) LAUNDRY FACILITIES ARE F HOTEL STAFF ONLY!
10) ANY AND ALL ODD SMELLS WILL BE INVESTIGATED--se rule #1!

HAVE A NICE STAY.

NO POWERS

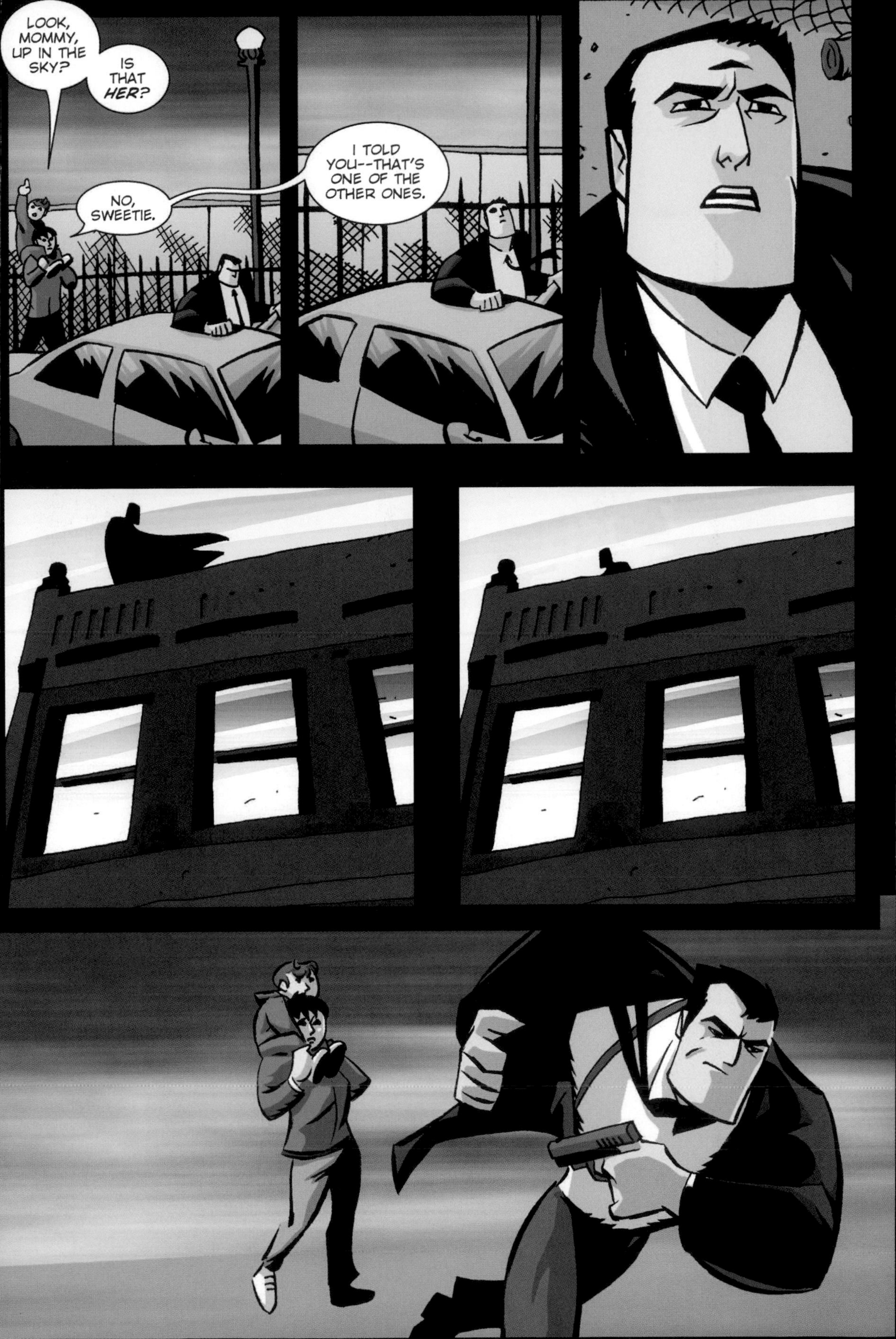
LOOK, MOMMY, UP IN THE SKY?
IS THAT *HER*?
NO, SWEETIE.
I TOLD YOU--THAT'S ONE OF THE OTHER ONES.

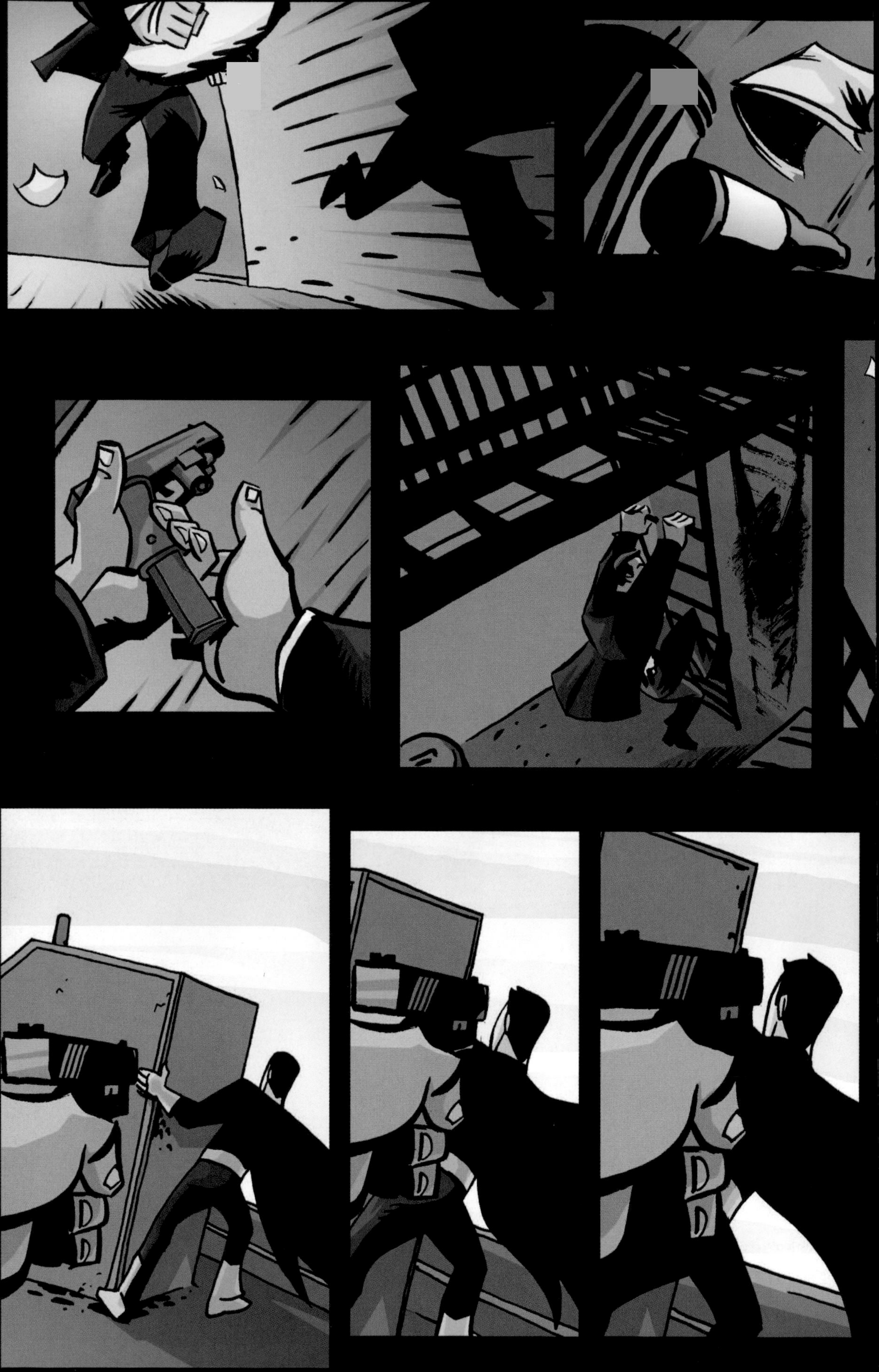

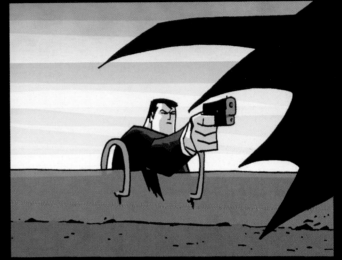

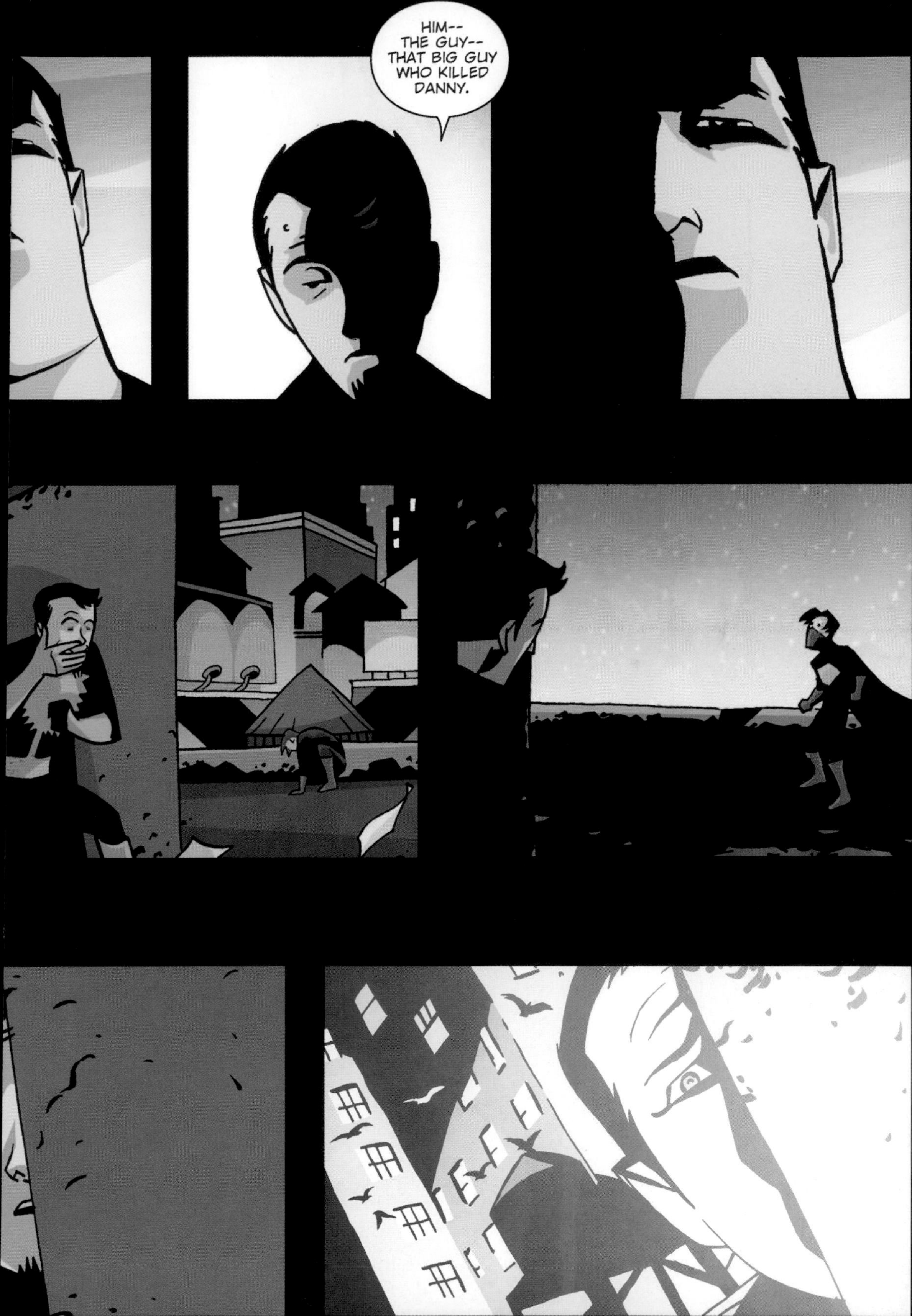
HIM-- THE GUY-- THAT BIG GUY WHO KILLED DANNY.

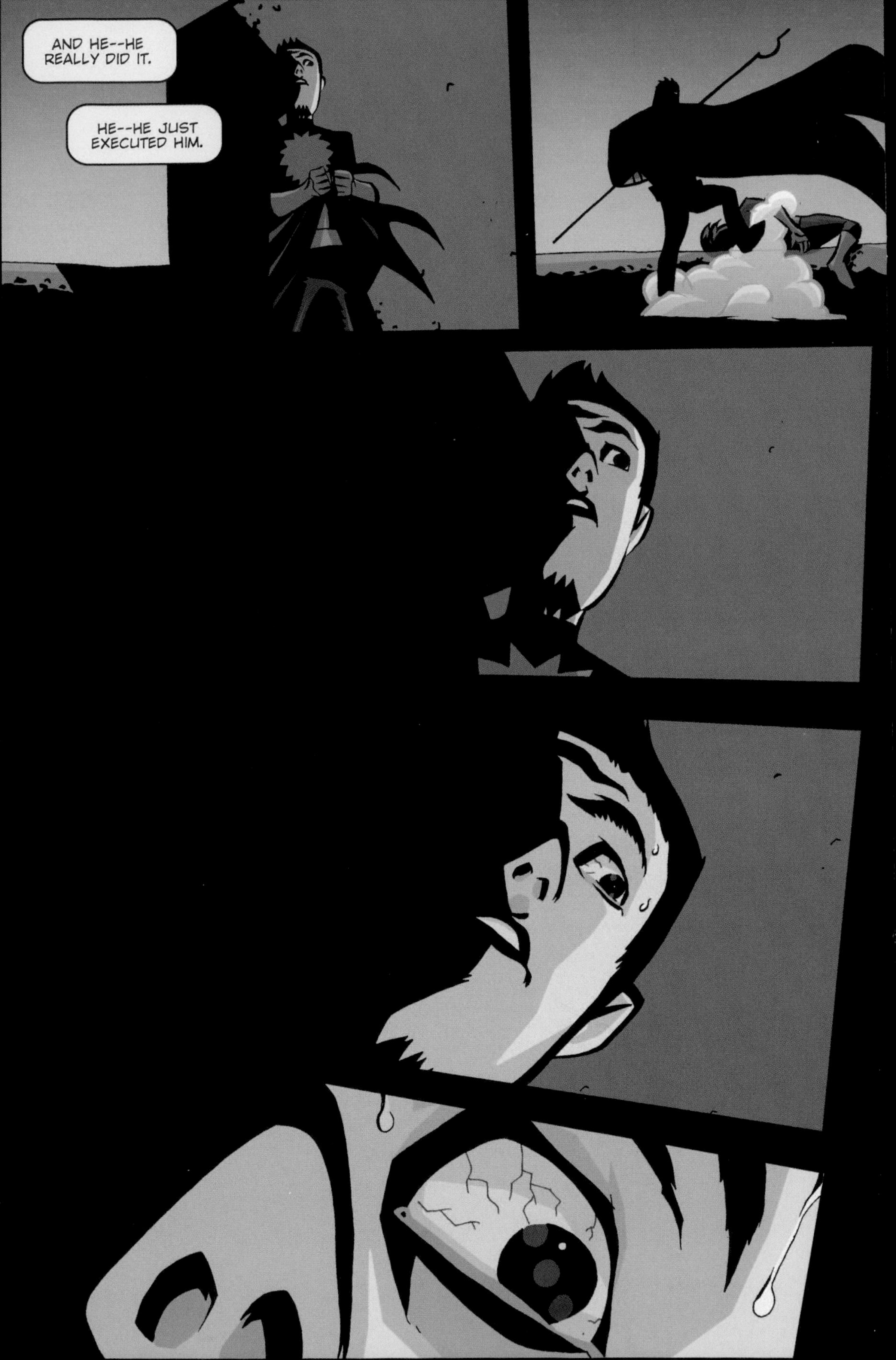
AND HE--HE REALLY DID IT.
HE--HE JUST EXECUTED HIM.

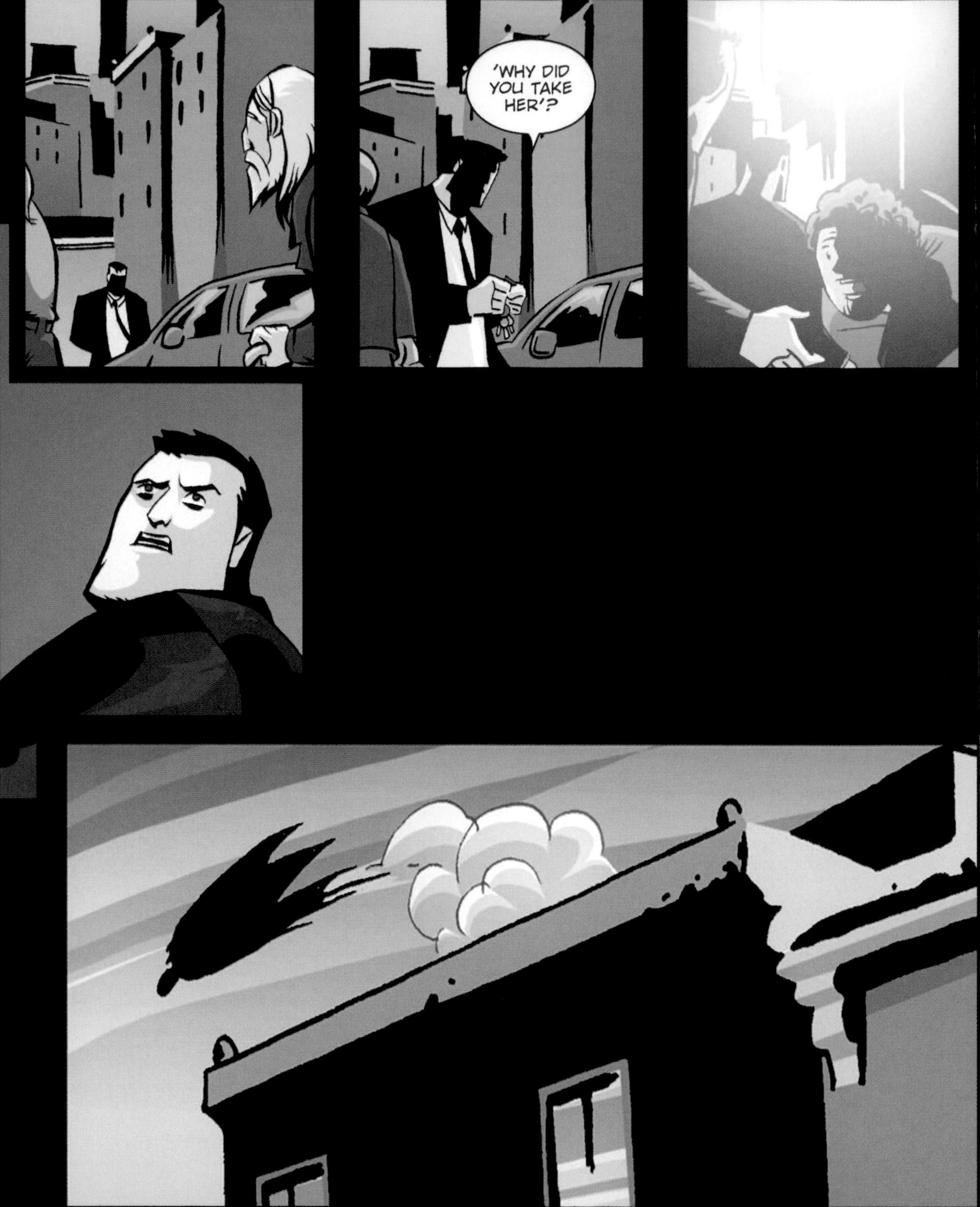
'WHY DID YOU TAKE HER'?

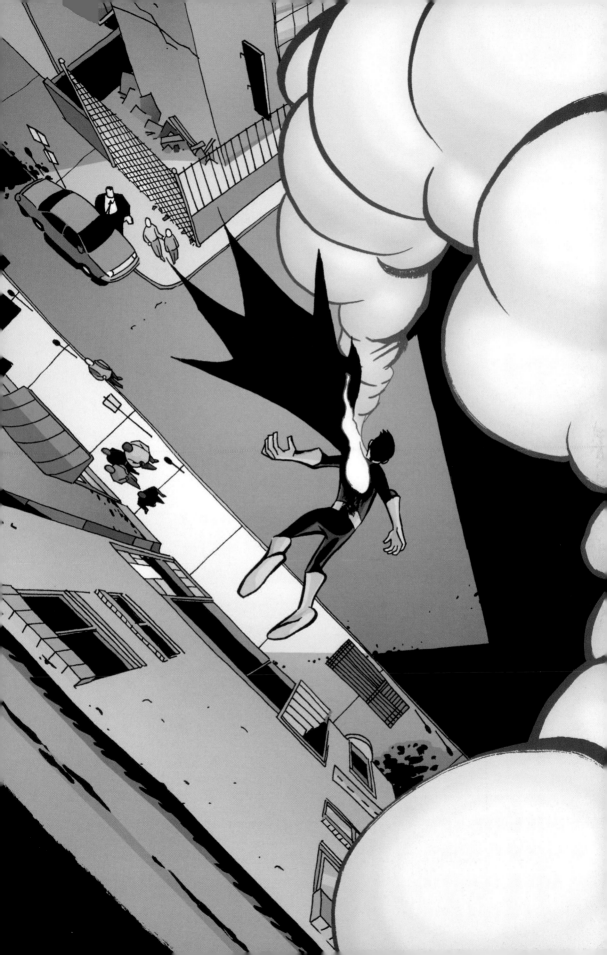

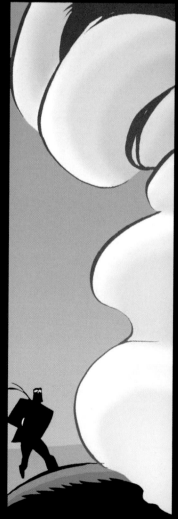

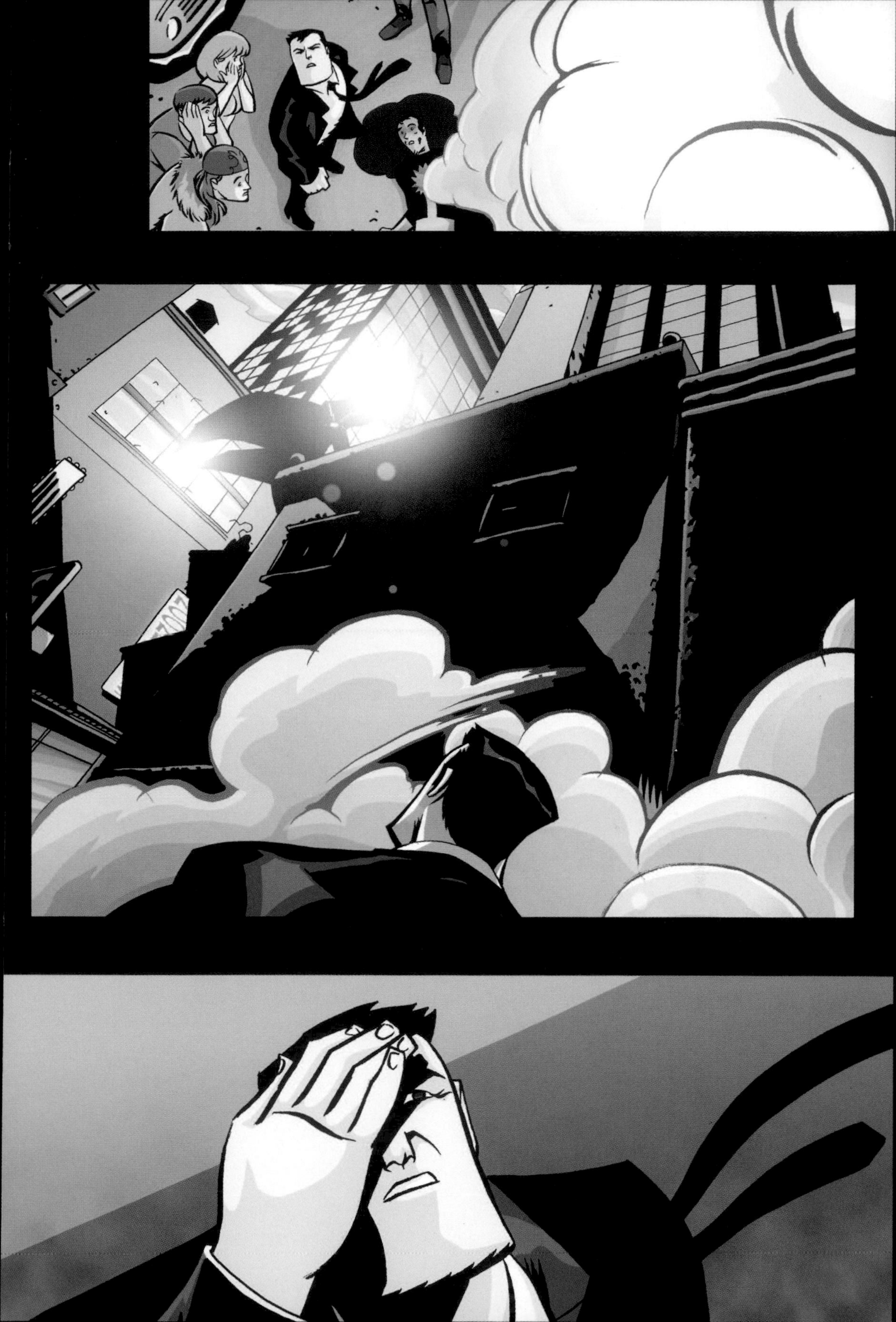

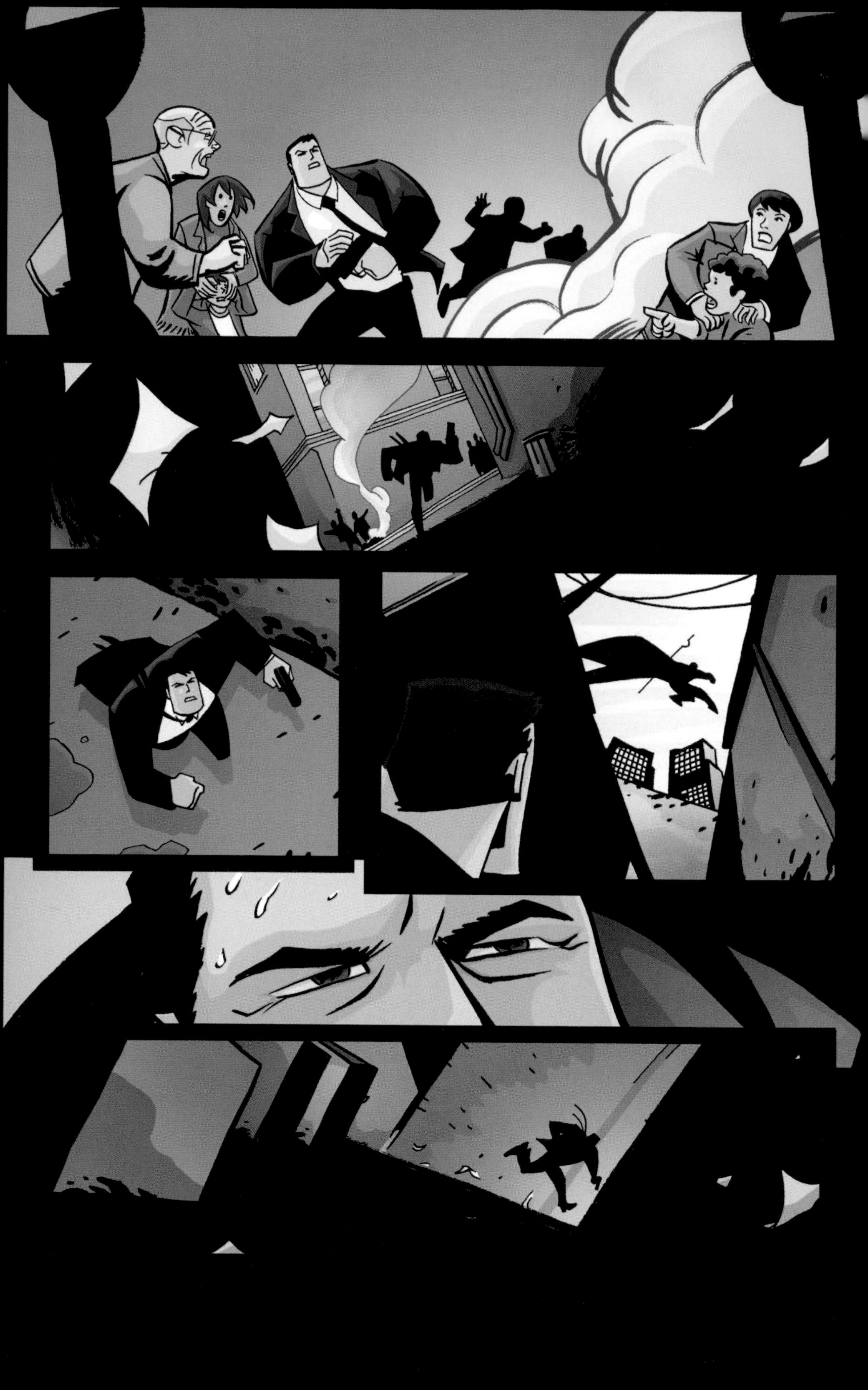

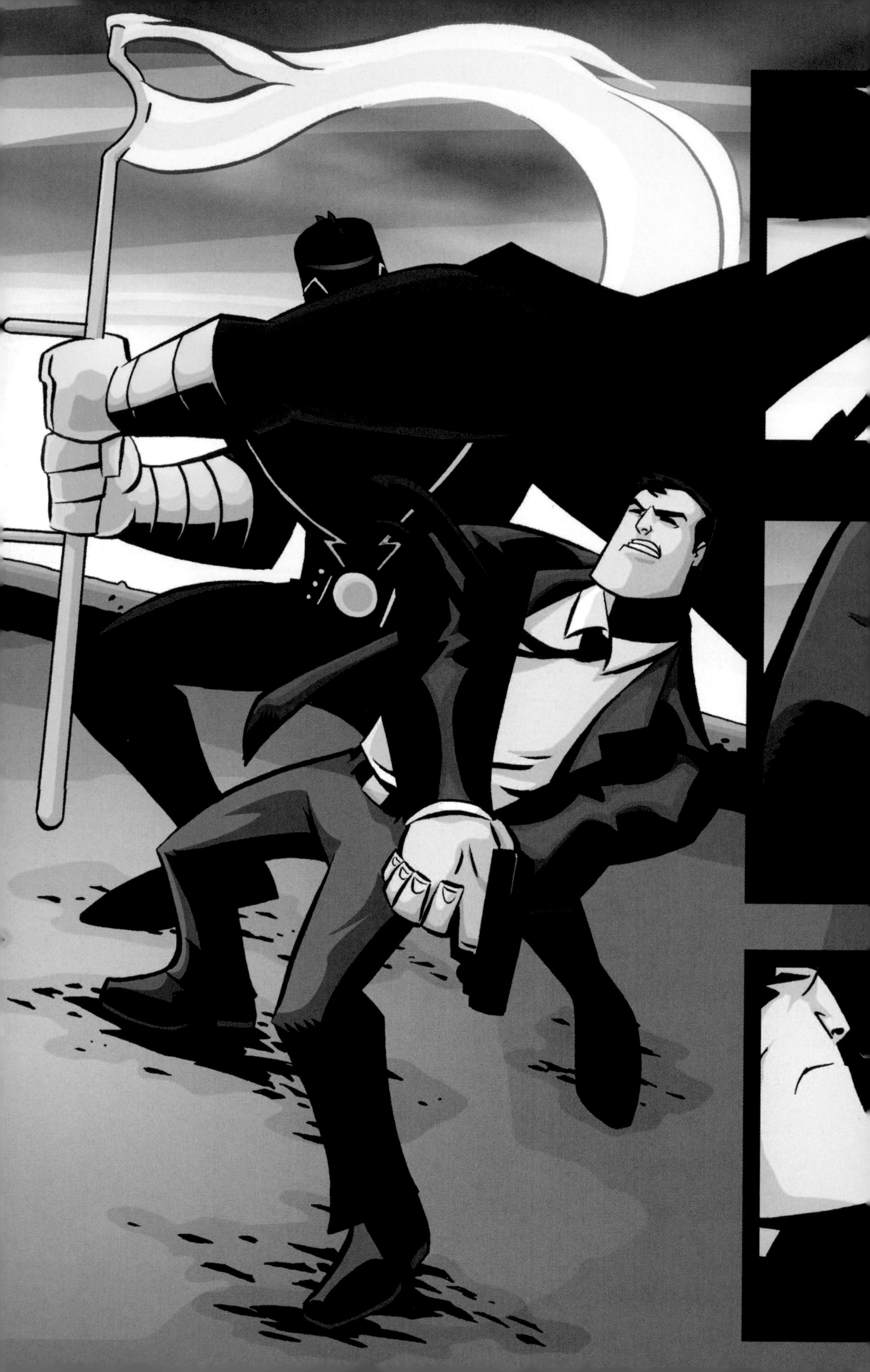

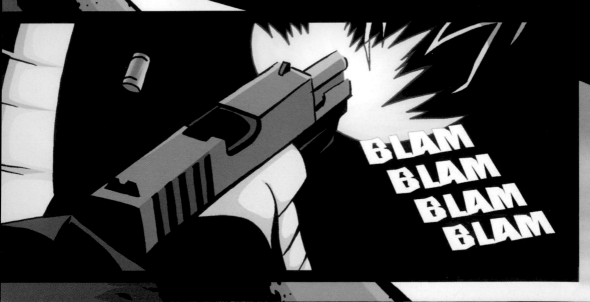

BLAM
BLAM
BLAM
BLAM

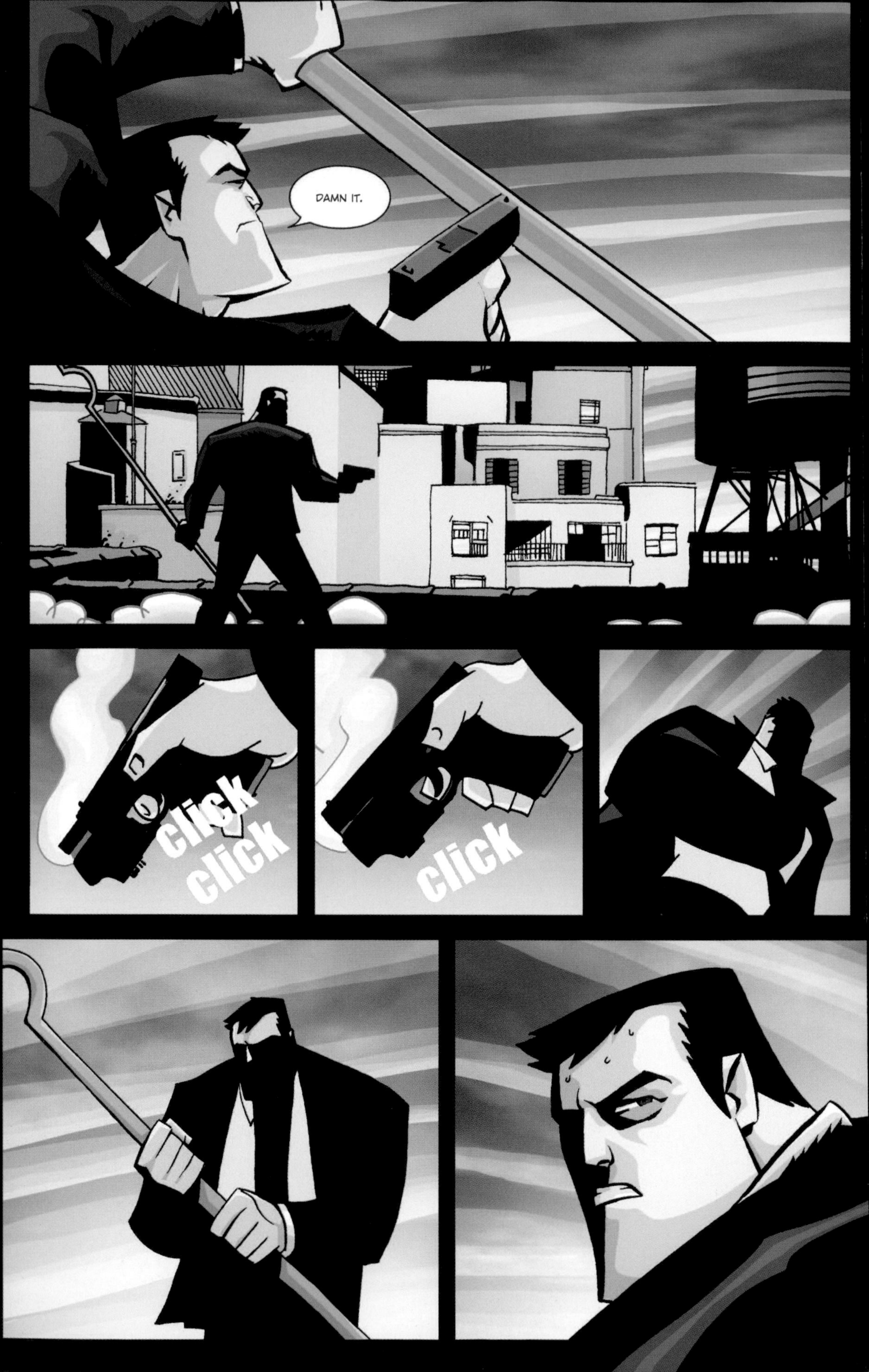
DAMN IT.
click
click
click

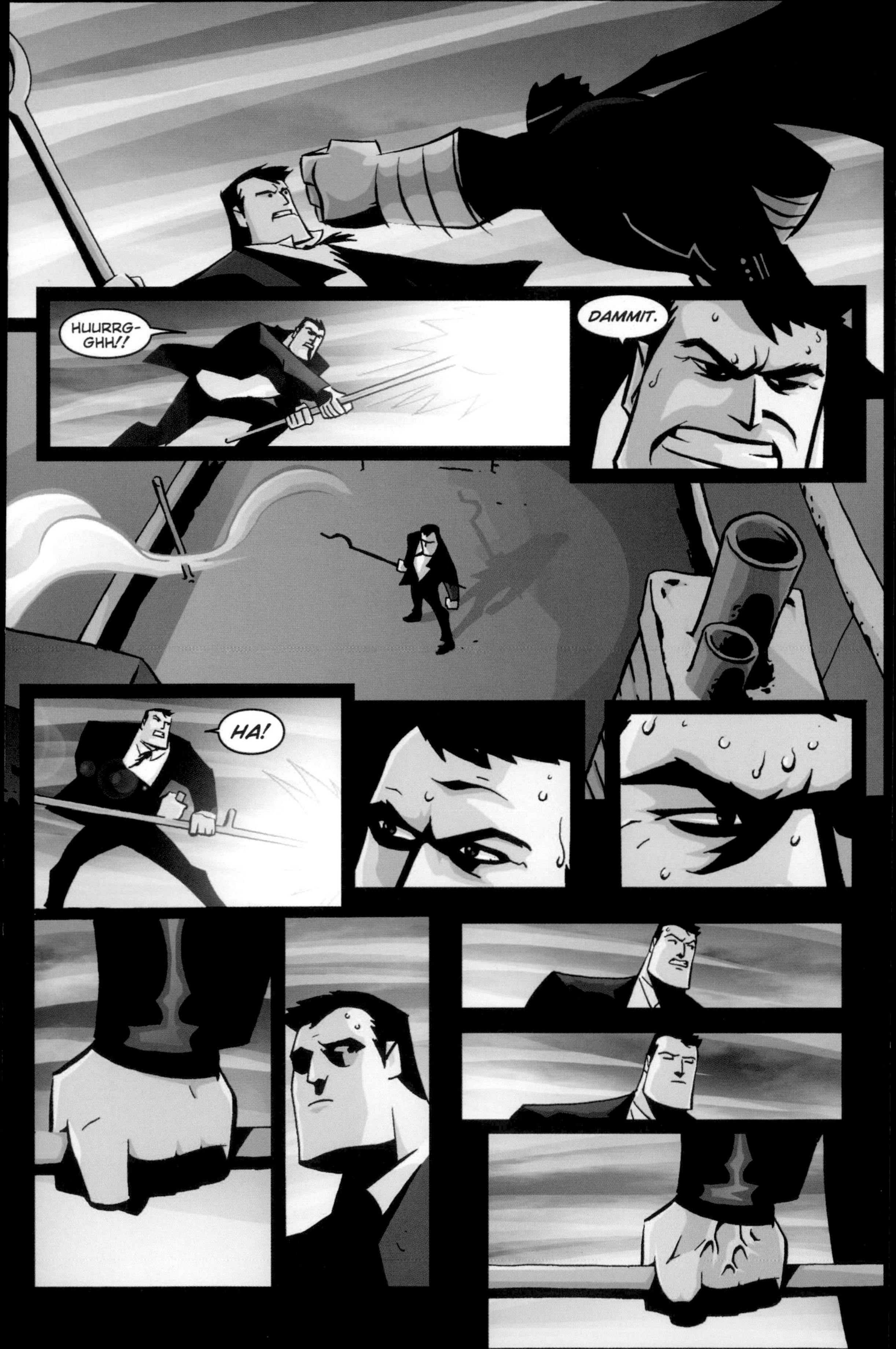
HUURRG-GHH!!
DAMMIT.
HA!

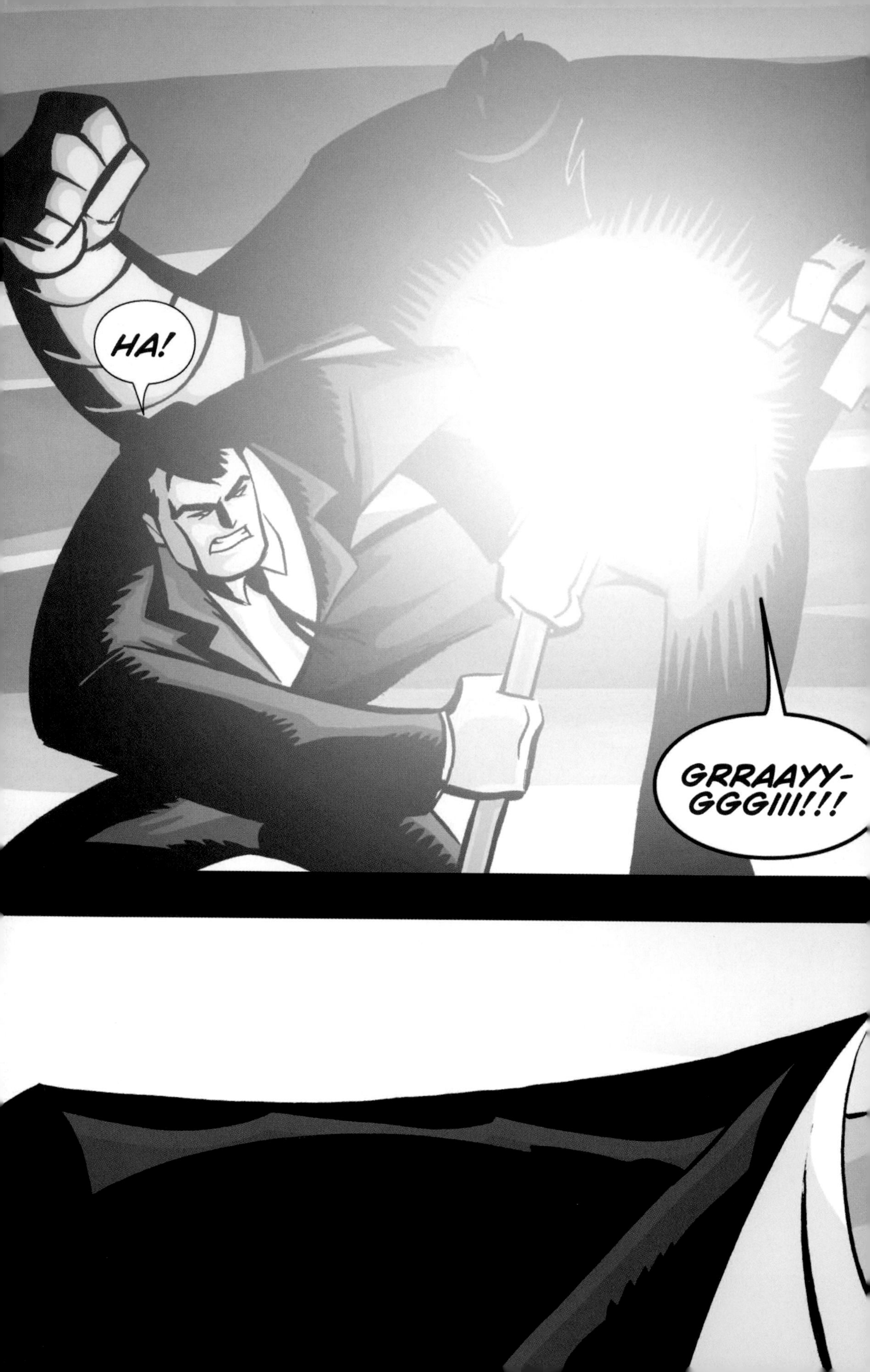
HA!
GRRAAYY-
GGGIII!!!

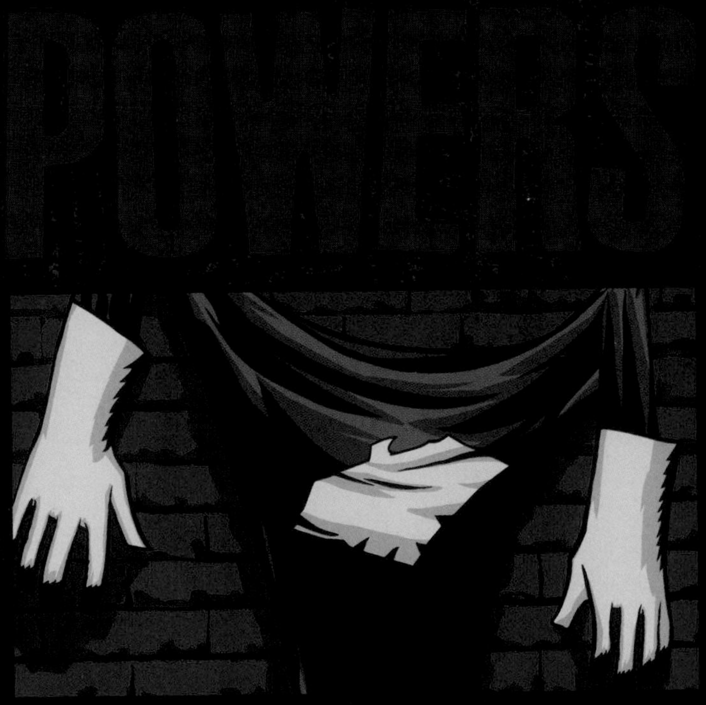
POWERS

COVER GALLERY

Ever notice how there's about five basic mainstream comic book cover designs? You know them:

1. The hero leaping at you, readying for battle.
2. The close-up of the hero grimacing at you, with the shadow of whatever villain he is facing cast half over his face.
3. The logo of the comic smashing from the force of the great battle going on underneath it.
4. The big maniacally laughing villain close-up.
5. Let's not forget, the ever-popular giant boobs smushed together in the middle of the cover with a couple of spots of blood on them that, at first glace, somewhat resemble nipplage.

These are what we call in the business: Comic Book Cliches. And if I am ever responsible for purposefully executing one here in Powers, I will kill myself, but then make it look like Mike Oeming did it. Mike and I decided very early on to create theme covers for each story arc. And for this storyline we ended up using album cover designs from albums you would find in a collage dorm room.

But the road to a good idea is not always smooth. There's a lot of really bad ideas pursued, or as Mike likes to call them: ideas forced down the artist's throat from a know-it-all writer. And then there are the cover designs created by an artist hopped up on paint fumes.

Join us now as we take you on a trip through the cover gallery, then onto the abandoned cover concepts and sketches. We hope that you will find it interesting, and by that I mean I hope the extra effort gets us nominated for something.

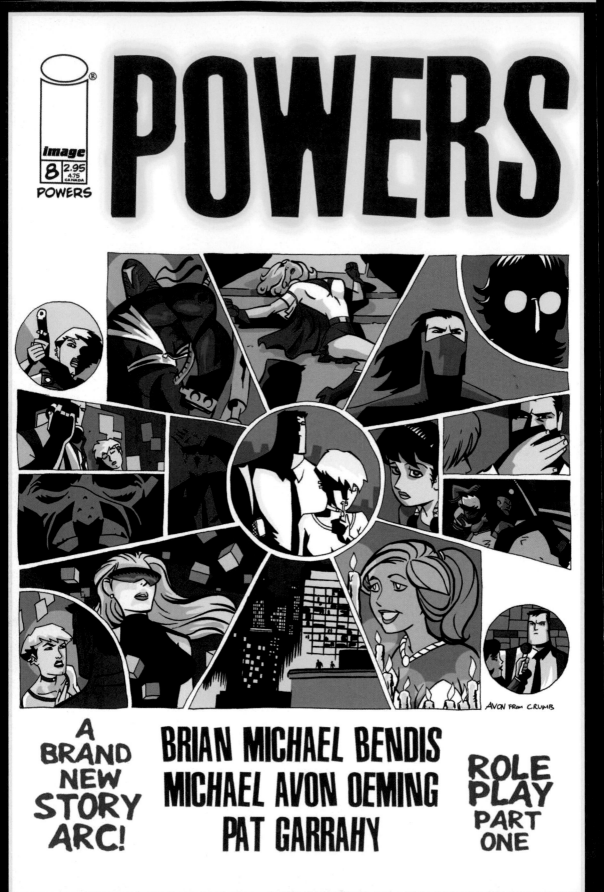

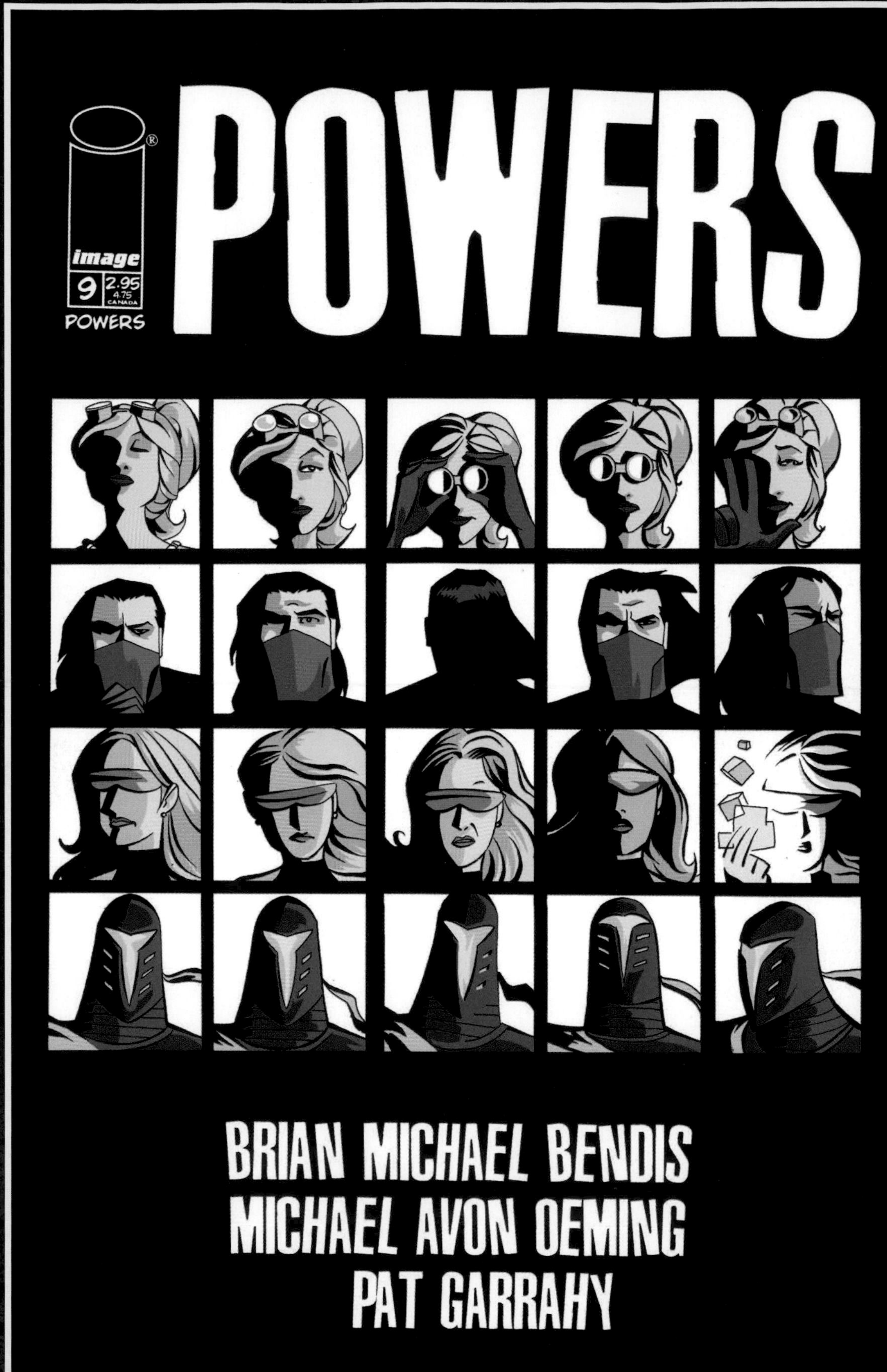
POWERS
image
9 2.95 4.75 CANADA
POWERS
BRIAN MICHAEL BENDIS
MICHAEL AVON OEMING
PAT GARRAHY

Based on the Beatles' "A Hard Days Night" British import single cover.

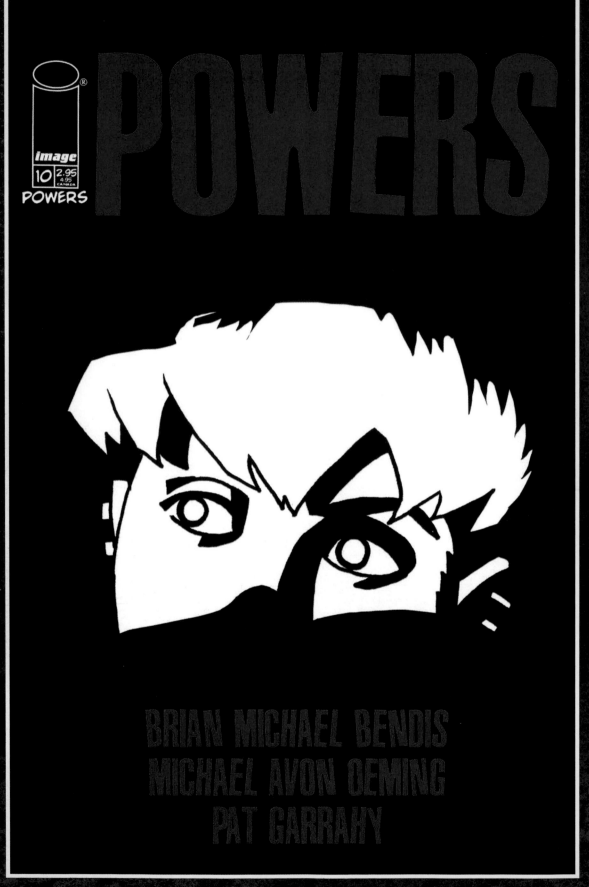

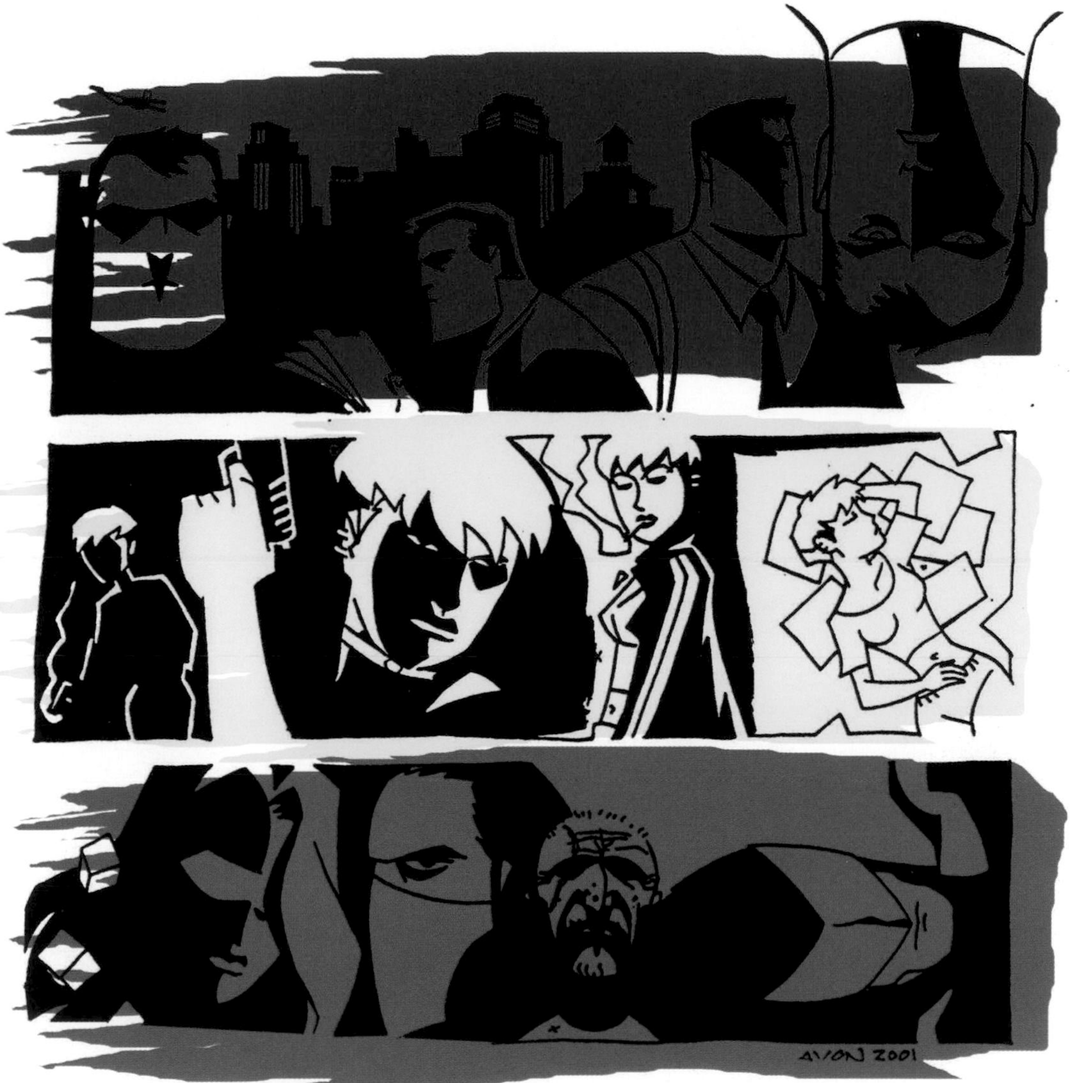
AVON 2001

Abandoned cover for *Powers* #10 based on the Police's *Synchronicity*.

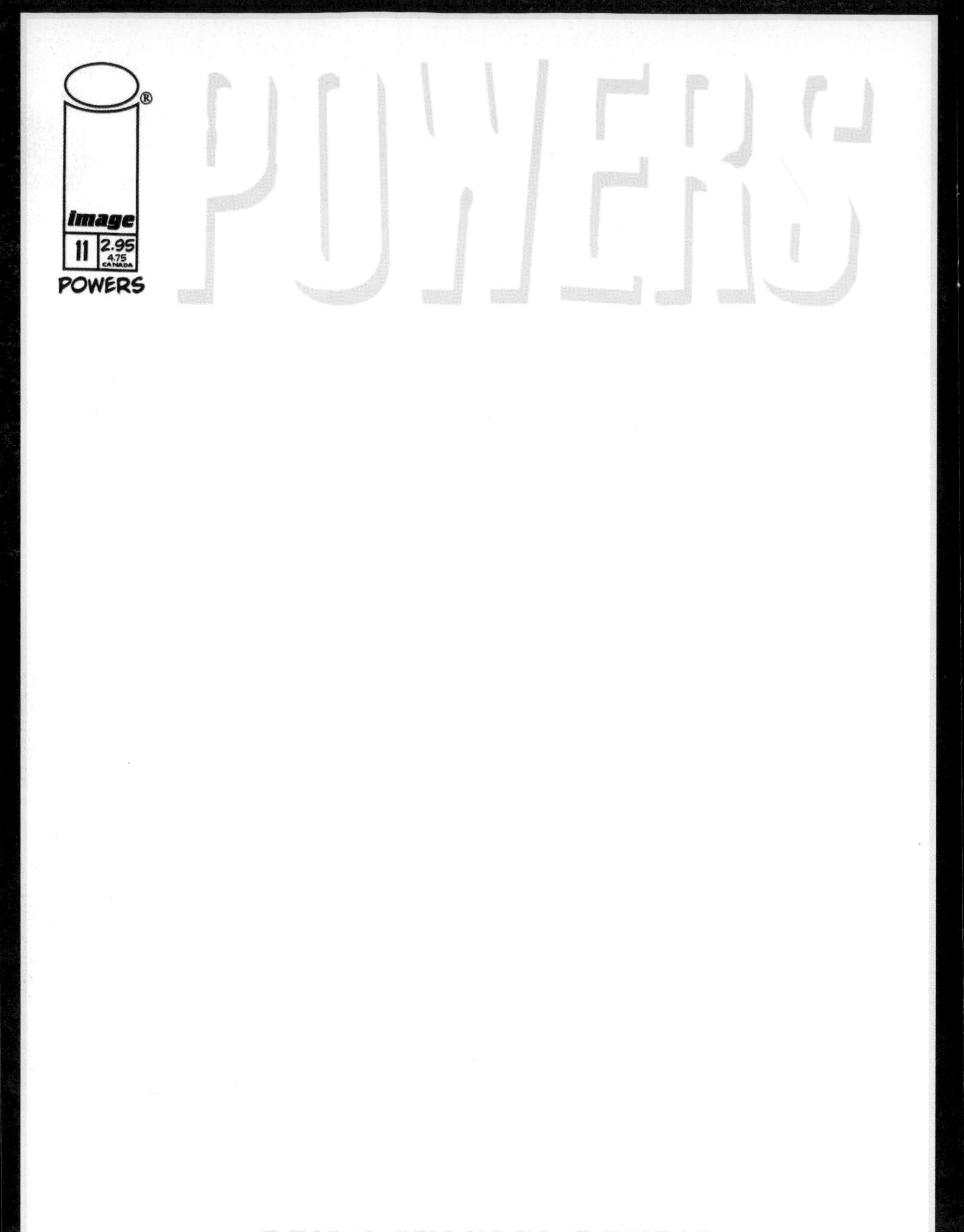
image
11
2.95
4.75 CANADA
POWERS
POWERS
BRIAN MICHAEL BENDIS
MICHAEL AVON OEMING

Based on the Beatles's *White Album.* (Duh...)

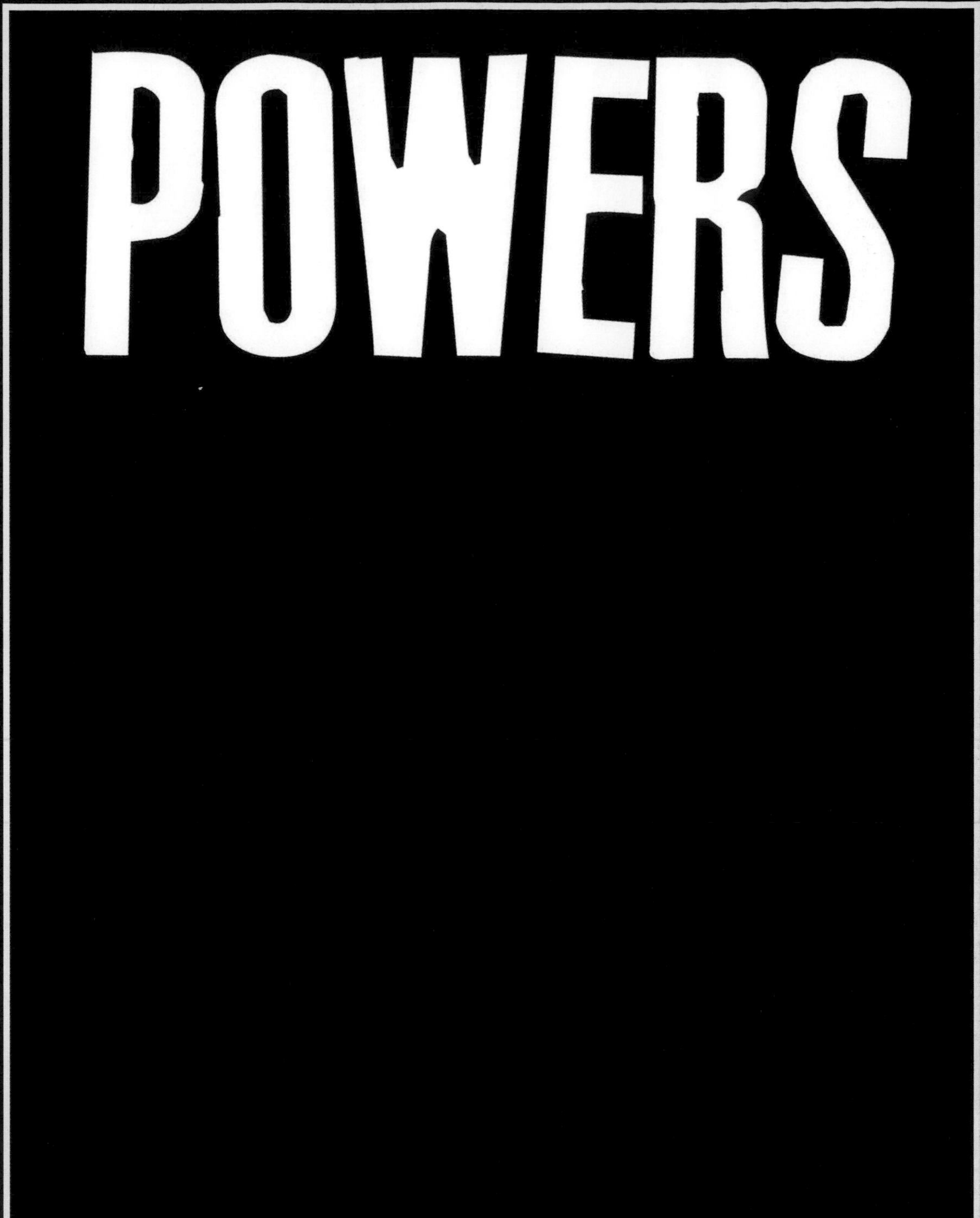
POWERS
brian michael bendis
michael avon oeming
image comics
2.95 usa

Abandoned alternate cover for *Powers* #11 based on Spinal Tap's *Smell the Glove*.
(It felt like we just stole the joke...because we did.)

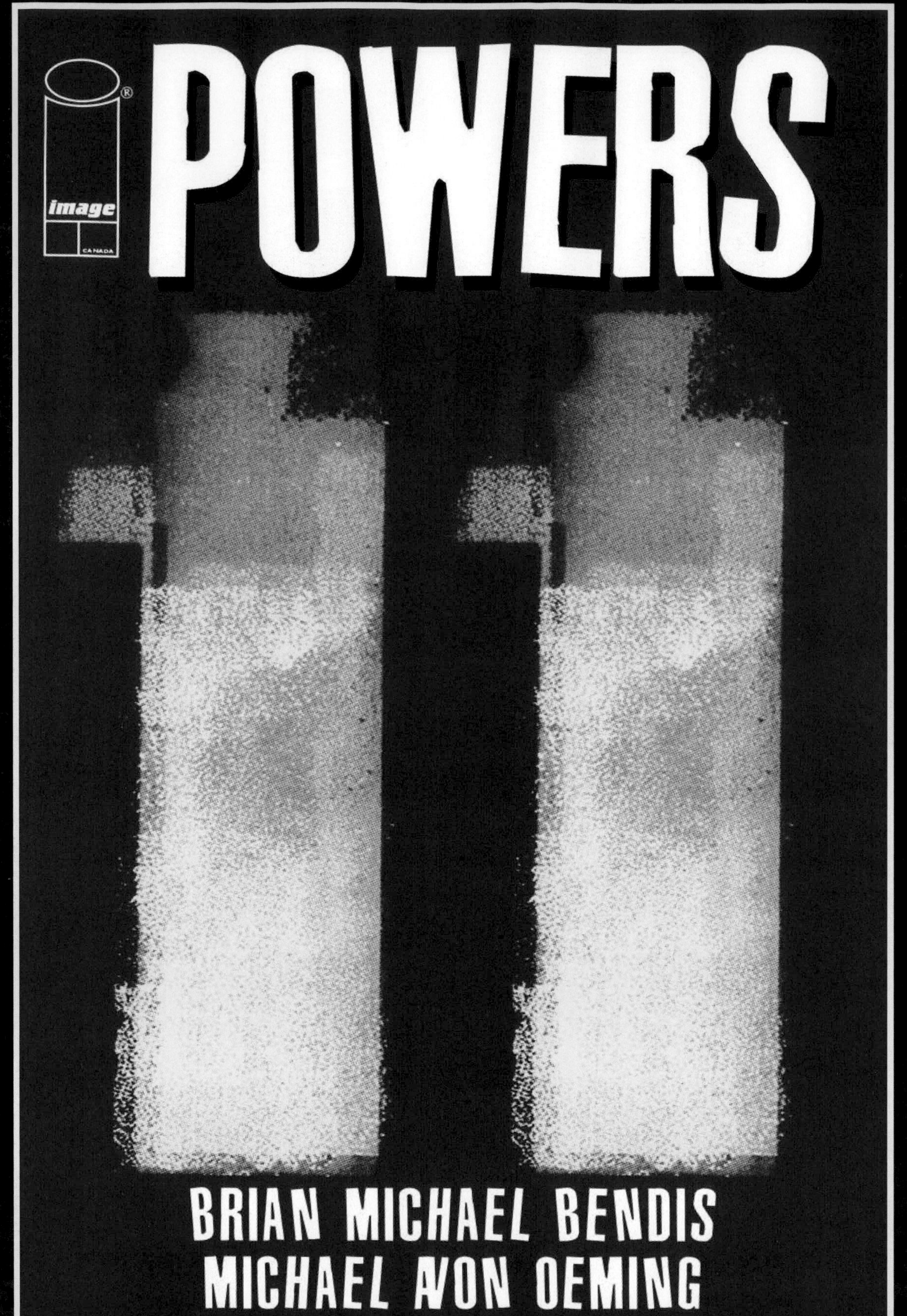
POWERS
image
CANADA
BRIAN MICHAEL BENDIS
MICHAEL AVON OEMING

Abandoned cover for *Powers* #11 based on the Beatles' *One* album.
(It felt like we just stole the artwork and altered it...because we did.)

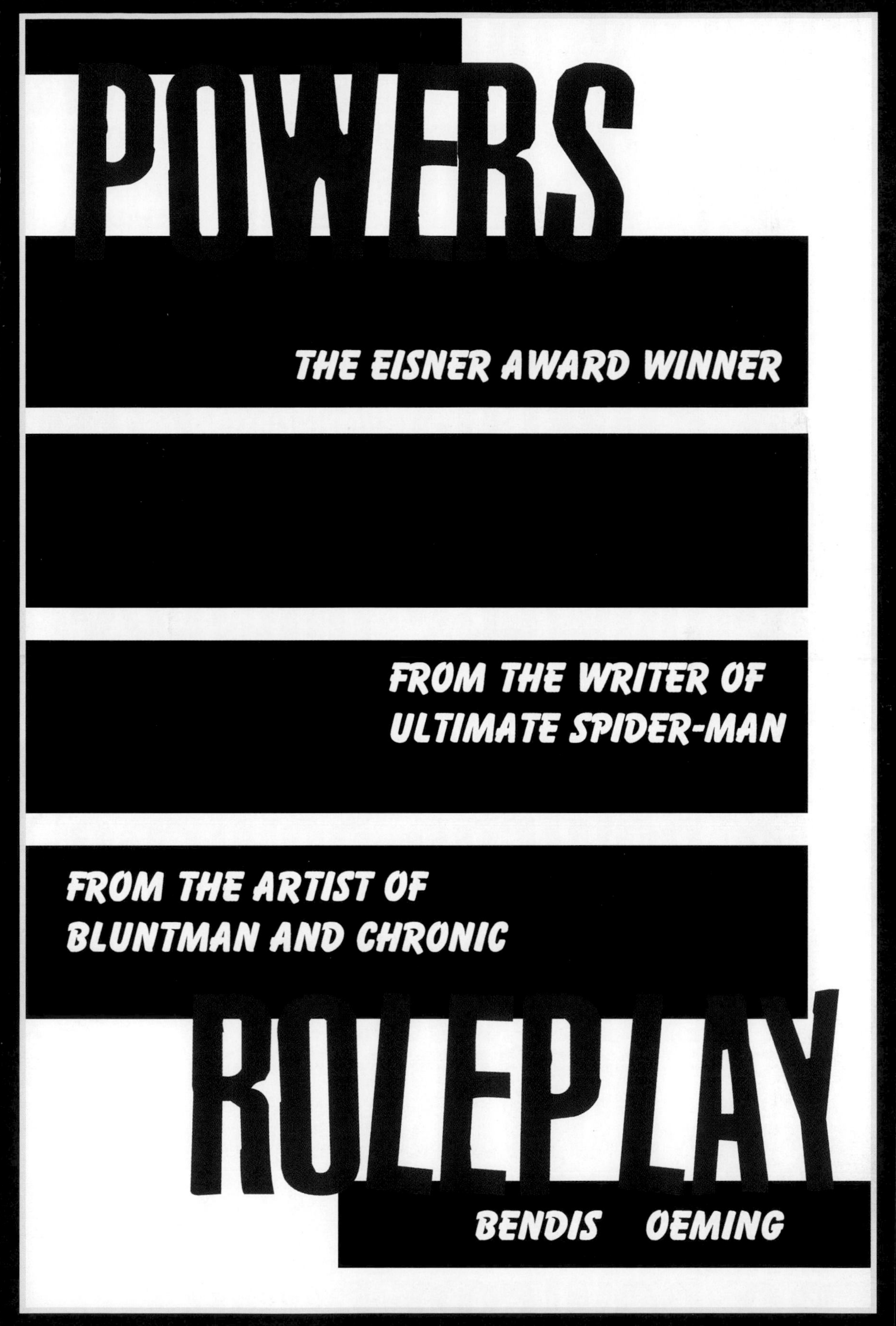
POWERS
THE EISNER AWARD WINNER
FROM THE WRITER OF
ULTIMATE SPIDER-MAN
FROM THE ARTIST OF
BLUNTMAN AND CHRONIC
ROLEPLAY
BENDIS OEMING

Abandoned cover designs for *Powers* using graphics instead of an image.
Not a bad idea but badly produced and it has nothing to do with the storyline.

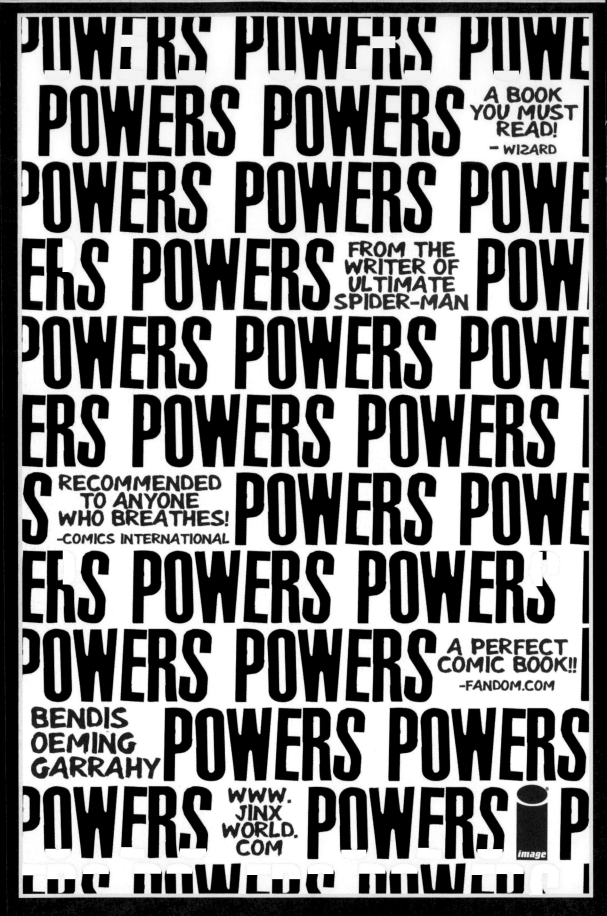

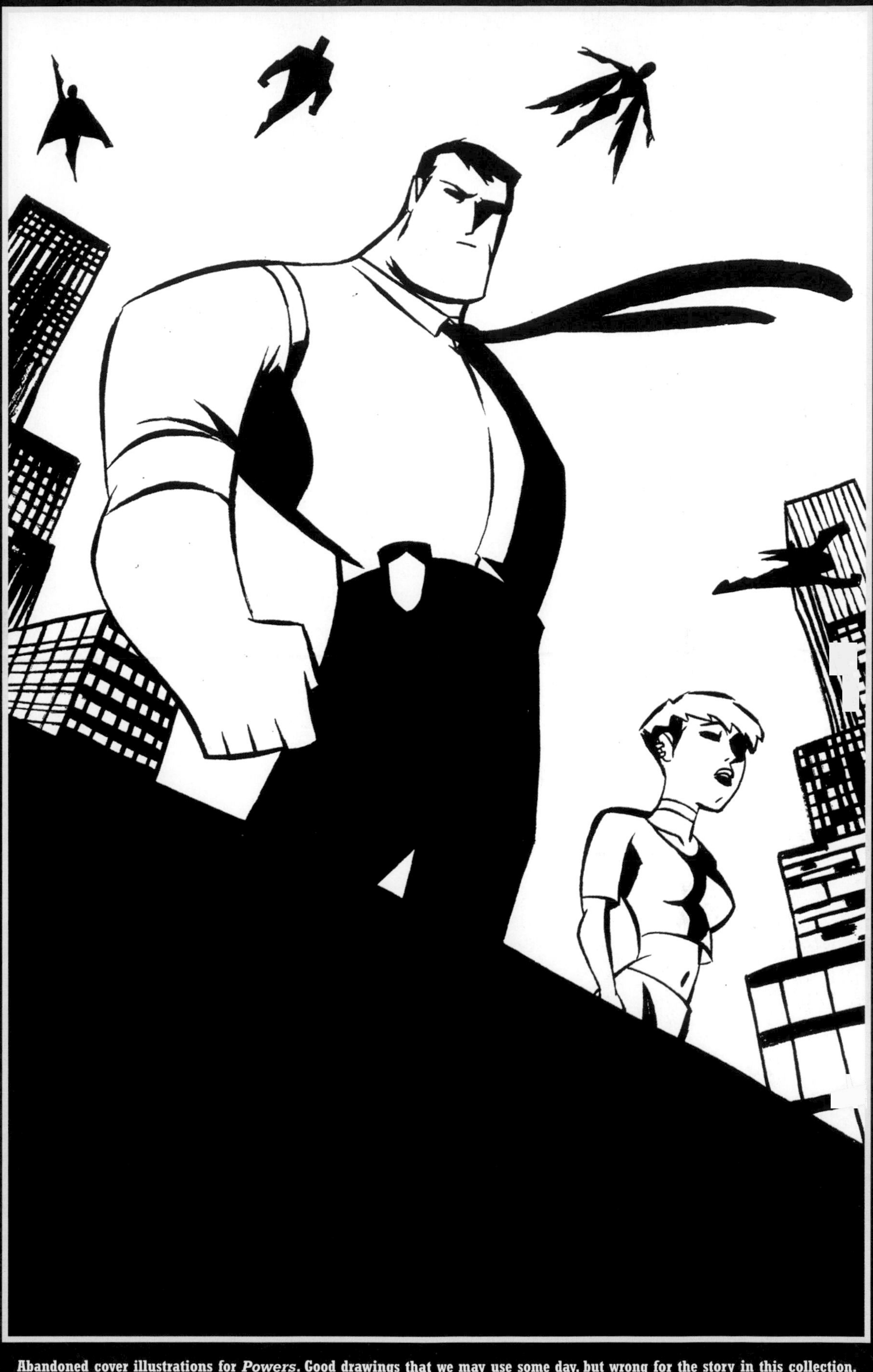

Abandoned cover illustrations for *Powers*. Good drawings that we may use some day, but wrong for the story in this collection.

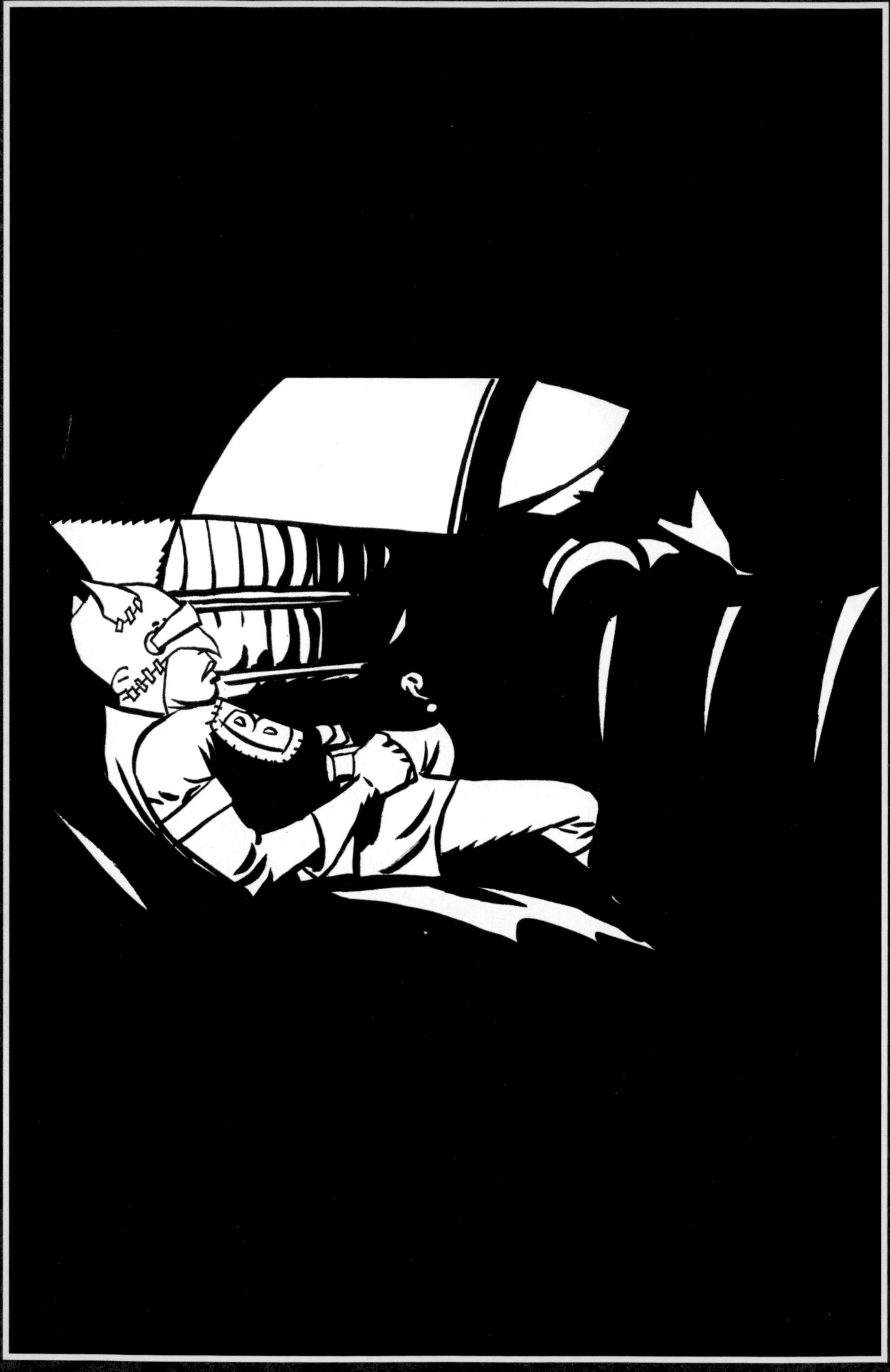

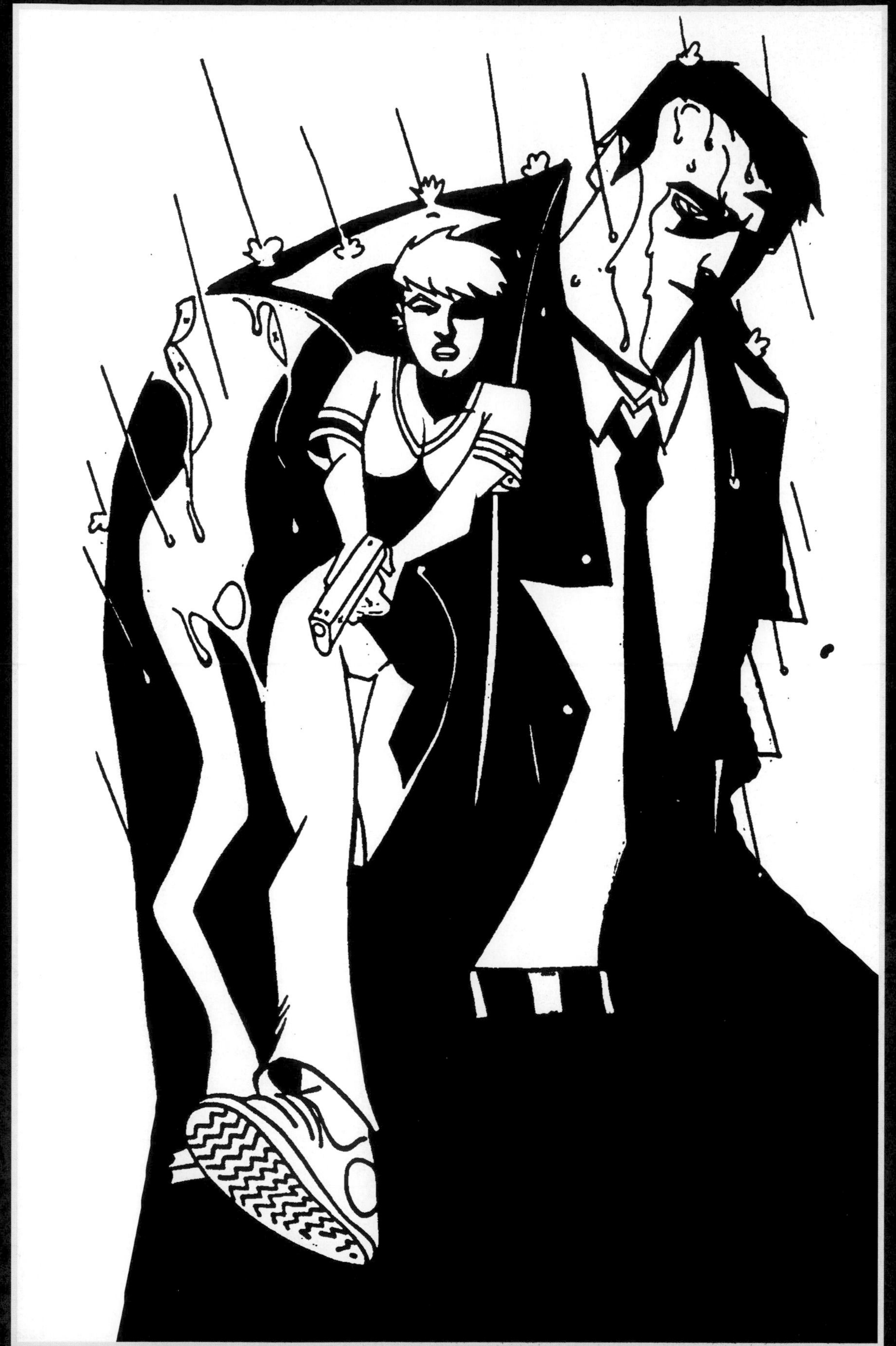

POWERS THAT BE
FIVE MINUTES WITH MICHAEL AVON OEMING

One of the hottest, most intriguing comics out there right now is *Powers*, a book that's taken the industry by storm. Following the beat of two human detectives investigating "powers-related" crimes in their superhuman world, *Powers* escaped from the minds of writer Brian Michael Bendis, who has had his own success as writer/artist with *a.k.a. Goldfish* and *Jinx*, and artist Michael Avon Oeming, whose work on *Ship of Fools* caught him more attention after his work on books like *Judge Dredd* and his superhero work.

The stylistic approach to *Powers* is very specific; in fact, Mike Oeming notes it was the impetus behind getting together with Brian Michael Bendis and specifically creating a crime comic.

"I met Brian Bendis years ago when he was doing store signings for *a.k.a. Goldfish*. We just clicked right away," Oeming relates. "We stayed in touch and talked about working together. After different projects came and went, I was looking for something new to do. I called Brian and was like, 'I want to do a crime book and I want to use this particular kind of style' — this Bruce Timm-ish/Alex Toth kind of animated stuff. And I really wanted to use it in a crime thing.'"

The artist explains the development of the realistic animated look of *Powers*. "The style developed from my trying to get work on the *Batman Adventures* stuff. I liked that style, but I couldn't stay on model, because I saw other things it had potential for that the series wasn't quite allowing. I really like stuff Timm was influenced by, specifically Alex Toth who was a huge influence on me. I just wanted to do some crime stuff using a combination of their two styles."

"That's basically what I told Brian," as Oeming affects a begging tone to his voice and says, "'I want to do a crime book with you 'cause you're a good writer.' And he was like, 'Absolutely!' We mulled over things. I faxed him some ideas. I didn't care what it was; I knew that we would just have fun on it. I assumed that it would be one issue or a couple of issues that would be released through Image central as a black and white. At the time, I had been doing *Ship of Fools*. So that's all we thought: little, tiny black and white book.

"It just kind of blossomed from there," Oeming explains. "Brian basically had *Powers* in its nutshell. He showed me the thing and I was hesitant at first. I wanted to do a straightforward crime thing. And I was like, 'What's this?' And he said, "No, no, it's not about the heroes!' So even I took some convincing and thank God I saw his way!"

Of course, as everyone is well aware — or if you're not, you are now — that little, tiny black and white book is a bit bigger. Oeming for one is taken by surprise by the success.

"I'm not sure why it happened," Oeming admits of the sudden hit. "I think a lot of it had to do with Bendis' fans. He's been doing these crime books for many years now. First it was *a.k.a. Goldfish*, which ran into *Jinx*, which ran into *Torso*, and then he started getting picked up for other companies to do books, like *Sam & Twitch*. So he really started building his fan base. So that and the commerciality of my artwork, it was what people were looking for, or at least people who hadn't read his stuff before. I think that's what I brought into the fold really, a certain amount of commerciality. My work's very iconic, you look at it and immediately know what it is, it's so simple. That's what I like about it. Brian's artwork is